PENGUIN BUSINESS

THE FINANCIAL INDEPENDENCE MARATHON

Vinod N. Bhat has more than fifteen years of experience in the financial services industry and is currently working as a senior vice president and portfolio manager at Aditya Birla Sun Life AMC Ltd in Mumbai. He has an MBA in finance from the Wharton School, USA, an MS in industrial engineering from Pennsylvania State University, USA, and a BTech in mechanical engineering from IIT Bombay. Vinod is also a chartered financial analyst (CFA) charterholder. As part of his work, he has been writing, speaking and creating videos on various topics, including investments, the current state of markets and future outlook, and mutual funds, for the past four years. His audience has been retail investors, high-net-worth individuals, independent financial advisers and mutual fund distributors, among others. He has conducted more than 400 sessions with them so far. This has given him a good understanding of their knowledge of the subject (or lack thereof) and the best way to communicate with them. He lives with his mother, wife and daughter in Mumbai/Pune. You can connect with Vinod on LinkedIn and Twitter.

T0017773

ADVANCE PRAISE FOR THE BOOK

'The definitive guide on achieving financial independence through prudent asset allocation'—Gautam Baid, founder, Stellar Wealth Partners, and author, *The Joys of Compounding*

'This book covers everything you want to know about managing money, planning your finances and understanding various asset classes. I loved reading this book, with each chapter providing clarity with actionable takeaways. Consider this book as a companion navigating you to achieve financial independence'—K.S. Rao, head investor education and distributor development, Aditya Birla Sun Life AMC Ltd

'Enjoyed reading this book. A nice storytelling format and an interesting pace to learn a few critical concepts in a very simple manner. The book is a very good starting point for those who want to understand the world of personal finance and, of course, anyone who wishes to be financially free'—Rohit Shah, SEBI-registered investment adviser and director, Association of Registered Investment Advisers (ARIA)

'This book is an easy read for anyone who is interested in learning the basics of personal finance. I liked the presentation and simplicity of writing. It is a must-read for beginners, homemakers, etc., as it will help them understand the basics'—Melvin Joseph, managing partner, Finvin Financial Planners, Mumbai

'Loved reading this book. It explains the various aspects of financial planning in simple, relatable terms. It provides an excellent perspective on what financial independence is all about, and what it takes to get there. Having personally gone through a similar marathon experience as well as not-so-good personal investment outcomes, this book is refreshing. It crystallizes what it takes to get there!'—Vijay P., investor

THE FINANCIAL INDEPENDENCE MARATHON

UNLOCK THE POWER OF YOUR MONEY

VINOD N. BHAT

BUSINESS

An imprint of Penguin Random House

PENGUIN BUSINESS

USA | Canada | UK | Ireland | Australia
New Zealand | India | South Africa | China

Penguin Business is part of the Penguin Random House group of companies
whose addresses can be found at global.penguinrandomhouse.com

Published by Penguin Random House India Pvt. Ltd
4th Floor, Capital Tower 1, MG Road,
Gurugram 122 002, Haryana, India

Penguin
Random House
India

First published in Penguin Business by Penguin Random House India 2023

ISBN 9780143459989

Typeset in Adobe Caslon Pro by MAP Systems, Bengaluru, India
Printed at Replika Press Pvt. Ltd, India

www.penguin.co.in

MIX
Paper from
responsible sources
FSC® C016779

To the community of investors, independent financial advisers and mutual fund distributors, for giving me something worth writing about

And to my family, for being the catalyst that motivated me to write about it

Contents

Foreword

Money is an Eternal Dream

There is a wonderful dialogue in the Hindi movie *Deewaar* where Nirupa Roy, playing the mother of the two brothers, asks Shashi Kapoor, the honest son, 'Your brother is not sleeping these days even though he has become successful. I am worried.' To which Shashi Kapoor replies, 'Money is a funny thing, mom, you cannot sleep if you have too little of it and you cannot sleep if you have too much of it either.'

Our relationship with money is like that. When we have money, we ascribe it to our talent and capabilities, and when we don't have the money we want, we blame it on luck and fate.

Money, investments, investment opportunities and the concept of finance have changed in the last few years. The world of banking with its myriad regulations and jargon was understood by a few. Today, apps have made money, investment opportunities, etc., far more accessible and better understood. This trend will only accelerate.

In the old days, money was a legacy instrument; you were either monied or not monied, meaning it was hereditary. Today, that's not true at all. In 2022, India has 237 dollar billionaires, a number of them who have made their money in this generation with the paths of talent, hard work and grit matching opportunity. India has the third-highest number of dollar billionaires after the US and China.

How much money is good enough?

One needs money for one's basic needs. One needs money for one's wants and one needs money for paying back debt.

India is not a country with a credit-card culture. As with everything digital, India has leapfrogged the credit/debit card mode and gone straight into the digital way. India's digital payment system will be the largest in the world and is estimated to be about 40 per cent of total payments in India today. There is still headroom for growth.

India has huge aspirations and confidence in itself. Every young Indian believes that tomorrow will be better than today and that he/she will earn more. 63 per cent of Indians want to take a loan to meet their wants and desires that include gadgets, holidays and cars. There is a new lifestyle in town and that needs money.

During the pandemic, we saw the rise of the young investor. Young people facing salary cuts and reduced bonuses opted to invest in the stock market to make quick returns.

Money is also a key element of stress when people don't have enough money or they are falling back on their mortgage. I have been debt-free all my life, and I would urge people to be careful about the debt they take on, as not all debt is serviceable. In the world of business, we have seen many Indian businessmen forfeit their companies when their debt to EBITDA ratio was way over their heads!

India has one of the highest levels of savings in the world, close to 30 per cent. However, the young are saving much less than the older citizens. India has an employment-to-population ratio of about 42 per cent. Only 10 per cent of senior citizens above the age of sixty have a pension or a rental income. So, one does have to think about the later years.

I am really happy that my friend and colleague, Vinod Bhat, has written this book with his own take on this aspect of money in our lives. Vinod is a very talented professional. While he has a finance background, Vinod is also good at strategy and understanding business models, etc. Vinod has a nice sense of humour, which he brings in abundance to this book. Vinod is a keen student of finance and his WhatsApp display picture (DP) is one with the high priest of finance—Warren Buffett!

I wish Vinod and the book all success.

5 September 2022   Shiv Shivakumar
Mumbai

Introduction

'Oh, that's nice, Bejan Daruwalla seems quite positive today and is predicting good things for you this year,' my wife, Roopa, commented nonchalantly as I was watching an interview on a business news channel some time ago.

'What are you saying?' I couldn't believe what I had just heard. 'You don't know who this person is?' I asked her as my temper started rising, which was very rare.

'What happened? What are you getting so upset about? He is Bejan Daruwalla, the astrologer, right?'

'He is Rakesh Jhunjhunwala, India's most famous and successful investor in the stock market. How can you confuse him with Bejan Daruwalla? That's just not done!'

'Oh, is he? He was making some predictions about the stock market. So, I thought he must be the astrologer.'

'C'mon yaar, at least get your basics right. You can't not know Rakesh Jhunjhunwala! He turned his initial investment of Rs 5000 in the stock market into a fortune of more than Rs 45,000 crore. He is considered to be India's Warren Buffett. And most importantly, he is now financially independent and by his own admission, answers to no one but his wife. He has earned his right to make predictions about the stock market.'

'Okay, Okay. I'll keep that in mind. And by the way, why don't you learn something from him? When will you answer to no one but me?' Roopa made her point and quickly escaped to the kitchen.

I shook my head with disappointment. I worked in the field of finance and investments and my wife couldn't even recognize the most successful investor in the country. Worse, she was still stuck in the world of fixed deposits (FDs), property and gold, and didn't have much awareness about investing in other asset classes like equity and debt, or investment products like mutual funds and exchange-traded funds (ETFs).

But that gave me the motivation to write this book!

So, who is this book for?

Well, if you don't know Rakesh Jhunjhunwala from Bejan Daruwalla, this book is for you.

Even if you can tell them apart, if you want to know why financial independence is important and how you can achieve it, and if you want to be knowledgeable about different asset classes as well as investment solutions and products, this book is for you.

What will you gain by reading this book?

You'll learn a new framework that covers asset allocation and the five basic principles of financial planning as well as the basics of various asset classes and investment solutions. This should help you make better investment decisions and complete your journey to financial independence successfully.

What is my key message in this book?

'Time is money.' But the opposite is also true, i.e., 'money is time'. Money, if used wisely, makes us free and gives us time to do what makes us happy. It is crucial to understand the concept that money creates time because time is a non-renewable resource. And becoming financially independent is like finding a hidden treasure of time. It's just like striking a gold mine because it gives us the ability to live life on our own terms.

The key is not to think of financial independence as a goal but as a marathon that we need to enjoy. An investment adviser can help guide us and avoid any pitfalls on the journey.

CHAPTER 1

Everyone's Marathon Journey: Financial Independence

The Reunion

'C'mon guys, let's gather in a circle on the lawn, as we used to during our school days,' Akhil called out to everyone. It was the twenty-fifth-anniversary reunion of the standard X batch of St. Peter's High School, Pune and almost fifty of them had come together at a resort outside the city. It was a nostalgic time for all of them. Siddharth had been looking forward to meeting his classmates, some of whom he would be meeting after twenty-five years.

'Okay, so we're all excited to meet each other and have had individual conversations,' Akhil, who was one of the reunion organizers, addressed the group as they sat in a big circle on the lawn, after lunch. 'But to start with, let's properly introduce ourselves, talk about our families, what we have been doing all these years, and where we are now. I am sure we will have a lot more to talk about after that.'

As each of the classmates spoke about themselves and their families, everybody listened with interest. There was quite a variety in the paths that everyone had followed and Siddharth felt proud on hearing about their achievements.

Everyone spoke about their families and especially about their kids with some pride. The discussion then turned to their kids' interests, plans for the future and what courses they were taking up. At that point, Asim observed, 'Compared to the school fees during our time, current school fees and tuition fees are fast becoming unaffordable for a large segment of the population. As parents, we now need to plan ahead regarding how we will fund our children's school fees, tuition fees and higher education fees as they seem to be increasing every year at a much higher rate than our income.'

Asim had raised a point that struck a chord with everyone else. 'Very well said, Asim. My daughter is in standard X now and her tuition class fees are higher than her school fees,' Jennifer agreed. 'And I am afraid to even look at the fees of the best colleges in India. Not to mention that some of my daughter's friends are already talking about going abroad for their education.

With the home loan EMIs (equated monthly instalments) we are already saddled with, just thinking about this new expense is giving us sleepless nights,' she added as most of the folks nodded their heads in agreement.

'And, it doesn't end there. We also have to plan for our kids' marriages and our own retirement. We are all above forty now and time flies fast,' added Akash, sombrely. 'I invested in real estate as I thought it would give me good returns. But it has been a disappointing experience as prices haven't really increased much over the past few years and the rent I get doesn't even cover the EMI payment.'

Naveen added a new dimension to the discussion. 'I quit my job a few years ago and plunged into entrepreneurship. But it's definitely not for everyone,' he cautioned. 'At one point, I had used up most of my savings and had to struggle a lot to raise funds for my venture. I wish I had planned my finances better,' he added.

'You know, I tried my hand at making money in the stock market but was not successful,' Sunil said sheepishly. 'I read quite a few books, paid for training sessions conducted by some traders who touted themselves to be successful, and thought I had a good feel for the markets. But I have only ended up losing money. Fortunately, I have also been investing in mutual funds for some time now and that saved me.'

'Tell me about it,' Ashish said. 'I have tried my hand at everything from real estate, stocks, and even crypto recently. I made some money initially, but doing it consistently is impossible. Everyone seems to be making money in stocks and crypto. But when we try to do it, it just doesn't work. I wish there was some system that would enable us to do it.'

After the introductions were over, Milind, who was the chairman of their batch spoke. 'Friends, I'd like to start with an update on our school reconstruction project and our batch's contribution to the same,' he addressed them. 'As we all know, our school's infrastructure and facilities needed an upgrade and we had started a fund-raising effort in that regard. I want to thank all our batchmates for their generous donations. Our contribution will be used to build a well-equipped computer lab. Our classmates, Meghna and Sahil, who are working with HP and Cisco respectively, have also offered to ensure that the school will get a good discount on the computers and networking equipment,' he said, amidst applause and whistles.

'Milind, this is great. But the school can't just depend on alumni contributions, correct? There has to be a more sustainable solution and better financial planning is the need of the hour. The school's finances need to be self-sustaining,' Sanjeev brought up a sobering fact. 'Can't we assist our school in that regard?'

'Thanks, Sanjeev, what you said is very interesting and, in fact, is a perfect segue into a special session we have planned for the day,' Akhil responded. 'The discussion has made it amply clear to everyone that financial planning is crucial in all respects. So, without further ado, let me call our very dear classmate, Siddharth, to take centre stage. As he mentioned in his introduction, he runs his own financial planning and wealth management business. He will speak to us on the topic of financial planning and the path to financial independence. Let's use this session wisely to educate ourselves,' he said.

Financial Independence—Money Creates Time

Siddharth got up to speak, amidst some clapping. 'Guys, we just heard that financial planning is crucial, whether it is for ourselves, our family or our school. Having big dreams and plans is great but flawless execution is not possible without having the finances in place.'

'Siddharth, I have a different view,' Samir interjected. 'We should just aim to do what makes us happy. Money will come. Money can't be the goal. I have always followed that philosophy and it has worked for me.'

'Yes, Samir. You are spot-on. To be clear, I am not saying that money is the goal. Being happy is the goal and money is just a means to that end. If you are lucky enough to be doing something that gives you happiness and also takes care of your financial needs, then there's nothing like it. But, for many of our classmates who are gathered here, and for a majority of the public, that may not be true.'

'Okay. Got it,' Samir gave him a thumbs-up.

Siddharth continued, 'That's why it's critical to understand that financial independence at a personal level is a prerequisite for us to do whatever we may wish to do that gives us happiness, whether it is pursuing our passion, investing in a business, contributing to our school, society, and country, or for philanthropic purposes.

'I wish this had been part of our school curriculum itself twenty-five years ago as it would have been useful for us in our life's journey. But, it's better late than never. And it's important that we understand this and also teach this to our friends and more importantly to our kids who are in school today so that they can do better than us, right?'

'Absolutely right, Siddharth,' Naveen agreed with him. 'I wish I had known about this earlier. But, what exactly do you mean by financial independence? Could you please elaborate on this?'

There were quite a few people in the audience now who were interested in knowing more.

'Financial independence is the ability to live life on our own terms. That's simple to understand, correct?' Siddharth asked as the group replied in the affirmative.

'To clarify, it doesn't mean reaching a state where you don't work and just retire. It just means that you don't need to work if you don't want to. It enables you to stop thinking about your day-to-day or short-term goals and instead allows you to focus on your long-term goals. As Robert Kiyosaki, the acclaimed author, has said— financial independence is about having more choices. It gives you the opportunity to consider your choices and select only those that give you happiness.'

'Okay. Let's do a quick exercise so that this sinks in,' Siddharth said. 'Let's all close our eyes for one minute, relax, and visualize what we would do if we were financially independent.'

'Good idea, Siddharth,' Milind seconded him, 'Let's do this exercise.'

Everyone closed their eyes, relaxed and sat quietly. After a minute, Siddharth asked, 'Who wants to go first?'

Rashmi was the first to speak. 'I love to act in plays and would love to do it full-time. But right now, I can only do it on and off as I also need a job to support my family. If my family was financially independent, I would pursue my passion for acting in plays full-time,' she said.

'I would definitely start my own business,' Shrikant, who worked at a bank, went next. 'I have had an idea to build a product in the fintech space for a long time and I'll pursue that.'

'I would focus on my organic farm full-time. I started it as a side project a couple of years ago and it has picked up really well. I think there is a lot of demand for organic products and it has good potential,' Sanjeev volunteered.

'I would like to be a venture capital investor. I like meeting people and discussing new ideas. Investing in new businesses will be exciting and I would like to support entrepreneurs like our own Naveen,' Mahesh was next.

'Monali and I would start a cosmetics business together. We've always discussed that in the past,' Smita said, as Monali nodded in agreement. They had been close friends since high school.

Hema was next. 'I am stuck in a government job. I am very frustrated and notice the same thing in people around me. But, most of us have EMIs to take care of. If I was financially independent, I would quit and start an NGO focused on mental health issues. It would help me make an impact on society.'

As others continued, a variety of things came up, from expanding existing businesses to setting up new ones, engaging in philanthropic activities, setting up a recording studio, starting a cricket academy, going on a global tour or just chilling on the beach.

Finally, Mihir, who was a vice president at an MNC said, 'You know, I would write poetry full-time. I used to do that even in school but as I got swept down the tides of time by life's responsibilities, that got left behind. I'd like to pick it up again.'

'Ha, Mihir, we all know that special someone for whom you used to write poetry in school,' Neha teased him. 'Who will you get inspiration from now?'

'My wife, of course,' Mihir replied quickly, as everyone had a good laugh.

'Very good,' Siddharth said. 'Clearly, many of us are stuck doing whatever we are doing because of our responsibilities, EMIs, etc. And there are a lot of things all of us want to do if we were financially independent. That should give you an idea of how important this is in our life.'

'So, let's see how exactly financial independence gives us more choice,' Siddharth continued. 'Becoming financially independent means we don't have to depend on anyone—family, relatives, friends, job, clients, business, etc., for anything. So, we can be the master of our time and schedule.'

'That makes sense,' Mihir said. 'Even though I am at a senior post in my company, my time is not my own. Until we have financial independence, our time is controlled by someone else.'

'Exactly. And that's a hindrance which stops us from doing what we would like to,' Shravan added. 'By making our time our own, financial independence also puts us in a position to exercise our choice. After all, what's the point of thinking of options when we know we won't have the time to work on them?'

'So, the key concept to understand here is that we have two currencies in our life—money and time, and they reinforce each other,' Siddharth explained. 'We were taught in school that "time is money". But the opposite is also true, that is, "money is time". Money, if used wisely, gives us the free time to do what we want. That's why money is important. Of course, there are a lot of material things and comforts that money can provide but those come second to time. As Warren Buffett said, "The poor invest in money. The rich invest in time."'

'Wow, Siddharth, I never thought of it like that,' Milind said in appreciation.

'And do you know why this is such an important concept to grasp?' Siddharth questioned the group.

'Because, time and tide wait for no one, as we were taught in school,' Monali answered.

'Exactly. In different words, time is a non-renewable resource,' Siddharth continued. 'And being financially independent is like finding a hidden treasure of time that we can use and devote to whatever we want to do in our life. It's just like striking a gold mine.'

Siddharth remained silent for a minute as everyone was lost in deep thought.

Towards Financial Independence

'This is very good, Siddharth,' Shreya finally spoke for the group. 'We learnt something new today regarding how financial independence can help us. But how can we work towards becoming financially independent?'

'Now that is the key question,' Siddharth replied, 'Financial independence is not just about delayed gratification and saving money. That's just the first step. It's about investing your savings wisely to generate passive income and grow your wealth. That's where proper financial planning comes into the picture, wherein you need to invest in the right assets in a disciplined manner. Everyone wants financial independence. But very few are willing to commit to the hard work needed to achieve it. We need to be among the few who do so. The key is not to think of achieving financial independence as a goal but as a journey that we need to enjoy.'

'But how can we develop that mindset?' Raymond, who was listening intently, asked.

'I have found that the best way for me is to just think about it as if I am running a marathon. We have been having a serious discussion for some time now. So, let me try and lighten the mood,' Siddharth said, as he started telling the story of the Tata Mumbai Marathon he had run a month earlier. Everyone listened with interest.

Takeaways

1. Money creates time. Financial independence makes us the masters of our time. It gives us the ability to live on our own terms and choose to do only those things that make us happy.
2. Financial independence is not just about delayed gratification and saving money. That's just the first step. It's about investing our savings wisely to generate passive income and grow our wealth.

CHAPTER 2

A Real-Life Marathon Experience

'As you all know, I am an avid marathon runner,' Siddharth began. 'I had registered myself for the Tata Mumbai Marathon—the full marathon of 42.2 km, mind you—and had trained reasonably well for the past six months. However, the day before the marathon, some unexpected commitments came up at work. One of my high-net-worth clients wanted to discuss his portfolio and investment options urgently. Not only did I have to go to the office on a Saturday, but I ended up working quite late.

'My plans to take sufficient rest, hydrate myself and do some carb-loading all went for a toss. I could only go to bed at midnight and had to wake up at 3 a.m. in order to get ready and reach the starting line at Azad Maidan near CST Station on time, by 5.30 a.m.

'To make matters worse, I over-compensated in the morning and took in too much of water and energy drinks to hydrate myself, leading to some anxious moments due to gastrointestinal issues on my way to Azad Maidan.

'"Nothing has gone as per my plan in the past twenty-four hours, I wish I was better prepared," I remember thinking and shaking my head in disappointment as I made my way to the starting line of the marathon, early in the morning on the third Sunday of January. In fact, I felt a bit tired even before I had started the marathon, leading to some doubts in my mind about whether I would be able to reach the finish line.

'But, the energy of the rest of the participants around me gave me a fillip and finally, I crossed the start line at 5.59 a.m. as one of the last participants to start the marathon.

'However, the moment I crossed the start line, I felt a transformation. After all my travails, everything was under control now and nothing else mattered any more. As soon as I took the first step, I felt a sense of calmness and joy and knew that I would finish the marathon.

'The time I started the race really didn't matter because the Mumbai Marathon, like other major marathons, is based on net timing, that is, a chip on the running bib is used to capture the time a participant crossed the start line and finish lines, along with the times at several intermediate points in between. So, I knew that I was not competing with anyone else and it didn't matter whether I started the race first or last. I just had to run at my own pace.

'Based on my research, I had decided to follow the Run–Walk–Run method suggested by Jeff Galloway, a renowned marathoner and running coach. And based on his training, I had finalized a 4–1 run-walk strategy for myself. What it meant was that I would run for four minutes, then walk for the next one minute and repeat that cycle for the duration of the marathon. The reason for doing so was to conserve my energy for the latter stages of the marathon.

'I started slow, got into my 4–1 rhythm and started enjoying myself. As per my plan, I crossed the 8-km mark at the Peddar Road flyover in one hour, crossed Haji Ali, and at the two-hour mark I was on Worli sea face.

'I was soon on the sea link, still following my 4–1 strategy and enjoying every moment. My favourite part of the Mumbai marathon is running on the sea link. The cool breeze is very refreshing. Normally people are not allowed to walk on it. So, running with the wind in their hair is every runner's dream.

'After exiting the sea link, I soon crossed the timing mat at the halfway mark of 21.1 km just as the elite African runners whizzed past me running at 20 km/hr. I cheered for them and was quite happy to reach the halfway milestone myself. But I also knew that the easy part of the marathon was over and soon the demons in my head would start playing their mind games. "Now the real marathon begins," I thought . . .'

Roadkill

"'I will not end up as roadkill," I repeated to myself as I crossed the halfway mark. Roadkill is a term most marathoners know well, and it usually comes into play in the second half. It is applied to marathon participants who end up sitting on the sidelines either due to cramps or exhaustion, or who stop running and start walking with no hope of continuing their run again. My goal was simple—"Run with a 4–1 strategy for six hours. Don't become roadkill."

'I was now at the Mahim causeway. I calculated that even if I ran at a comfortable 7 km per hour for the remaining 21 km, I would finish the marathon within five hours and forty-five minutes. The key was to stick to my 4–1 plan and not stop running.

'I was still doing my calculations in my mind when I saw my favourite heroine, Vidya Balan, in the crowd. She seemed to be craning her neck anxiously looking for someone. Seeing Vidya made an immediate impact and brought me out of my reverie. I puffed up my chest and poured some water on my face to look fresh. After all, how could I let her know that I was even a little bit tired? I waved to Vidya and to my surprise, she waved back. There was a relieved grin on her face as I made my way towards her.

"'Why are you so late?" she asked me. "I was wondering whether you had fainted somewhere along the way. Those African runners had passed this point almost an hour ago!"

'This couldn't be Vidya. I took a closer look and sure enough, it was not Vidya Balan but my wife, Shraddha, standing there with a bit of concern on her face! Talk about the mind playing games during a marathon. *My glucose levels must be low, causing a brain fade,* I thought to myself as I stopped to meet her.

'I had requested Shraddha to stand at that point with energy gels, protein bars and energy drink bottles so that I could replenish myself. After collecting what I needed from Shraddha, I waved her goodbye and continued on my run. I was a little behind schedule but more confident now since my nutrition and energy drinks were in place to last me till the finish line. As I crossed the 26-km mark, I started seeing them—roadkill.'

Mind Games

'As I ran to the 26-km mark in Worli, I saw a number of runners sitting on the pavement or in bus stops clutching their cramped-out thighs, calves or feet, or just looking dazed without knowing what to do. Some folks were exhausted but were trying to walk with their head down hoping to finish the marathon somehow.

'Happy with myself for having run with discipline, I continued my relentless 4–1 march and reached the 28-km mark when unexpectedly, disaster struck.

'Out of nowhere, I felt cramps in the toes of my left leg. I immediately stopped, ate some rock salt that I was carrying and as if by magic, the cramps went away.

But when I started to run, the cramps came back. My strength seemed to have deserted me and my legs just didn't seem to be able to move forward any more.

'I had no idea what to do then. I had followed my running strategy with military discipline. I had followed my hydration and nutrition plan to the T. I had used the rock salt treatment to overcome cramps. Nothing in my research had prepared me for this situation, which I knew was due to inadequate training. My mind was giving up and it was taking my body down with it. I knew that I had to come up with something quickly or this was going to be the end of my Mumbai marathon . . .'

The Wall

'*The Wall separates the worthy from the pretenders. You have to overcome the Wall to cross the full marathon finish line.* I remembered what I had read many times before in the experiences other marathoners had recounted about their runs.

'One usually came face-to-face with the Wall at the 32–33-km mark. It was the point when one felt that one's strength had been completely drained out because all the carbohydrate reserves were used up and the body was not able to quickly process the fat reserves it had. That's when folks typically got the feeling that they may faint. In addition, lactic acid built up in the leg muscles to the point where the muscles couldn't function any more, and one got cramps and couldn't take a single step.

Most runners had difficulty coming back once they hit the Wall.

'I was mentally prepared and was expecting the Wall at the 32–33-km mark and had planned to slow down and run very carefully after 31 km. However, due to my inadequate training, I was facing the Wall 3–4 km earlier, and that too when I was least expecting it. That had thrown me off for a few minutes. I needed to think clearly and come up with an alternate strategy fast. I looked around and saw a water station just around a U-turn at the 29-km mark. I knew I needed to reach that water station and made my way towards it.

'There were some volunteers with ice packs and pain-relieving sprays. I waited for my turn and got both my legs iced and sprayed with a pain reliever. My legs were feeling much stronger now and more importantly, my mind felt calm again.

'I started running slowly and the Wall didn't appear again! When I reached 34 km, I felt that I had a clear path to reach the finish line. I remembered Eluid Kipchoge, the world's best and fastest marathoner's quote, "Only the disciplined are free" and knew that I just needed to keep running with discipline.

'So, with steely resolve, I continued to push ahead ...'

Towards The Finish

'Reaching the 36-km mark around the fifth hour gave me a big adrenaline rush. I knew nothing could stop me now. I rewarded myself with my last energy gel and a bite of the protein bar and pushed ahead.

'I switched back to my 4–1 run-walk strategy and began running freely as fast as I could. My body seemed to have found a hidden source of energy. Most of the fit and well-trained athletes and runners had already finished by then. 95 per cent of the remaining participants were just walking to try and finish the marathon. Some tried to run for a few steps but gave up and went back to walking. I was among the few who were still running.

'I had based my entire run on conserving energy for the last stretch and although I did have to face the Wall, my strategy was paying off now, exactly as mentioned in all the marathon stories I had read. I was crossing hundreds of participants now and the adrenaline was pushing me to keep going.

'After some time, I was back on Marine Drive. I didn't stop running and kept overtaking many participants on the way. At one point, I saw that for half a kilometre ahead, only I and two other participants were running, and everyone else was just walking. It gave me a big high to see that my strategy was paying off and I hadn't become roadkill.

'I crossed 40 km in just under five hours, thirty minutes. There was a huge crowd cheering from the sidelines as I reached the 41-km mark, which led to my anticipation building up. I wanted to run faster but decided to wait for the last 100 metres. When I reached 42 km, the feeling was indescribable. Only 200 metres to go!

'I finished the race with élan, running the last 100 metres strongly and crossing the finish line with a big smile and my arms aloft for the photo. My timing was 5:44:11.'

Over the Finish Line

'After the finish, I picked up my medal and goodie bag. I made my way home and proudly showed off the medal to my family. My daughter was over the moon. My wife, Shraddha, had reached home earlier and had been following my progress on the Internet using my bib number. I thanked her and told her that if she hadn't been there at the 24-km mark with my replenishments, I wouldn't have been able to overcome the Wall.

'My parents and sisters were thrilled to see my medal too, especially when I told them how I had overcome my cramps and made it to the finish line. They commended me for my never-say-die attitude. I put my medal around my dad's neck. He had not been keeping well for some time and the pride and child-like joy on his face will remain etched in my mind for a long time. It was as if my dad himself had run the marathon and successfully crossed the finish line.

'As I took a well-deserved rest and reflected on my run, I realized that completing a marathon and getting a medal was a worthy goal. But there were a lot of learnings for me from my run, right from preparation to execution.'

The Marathon as an Analogy

'So, what do you think? Why was I able to finish the marathon?' Siddharth asked his classmates.

'Because, in spite of all the issues you faced, you enjoyed your run and were determined to finish it,' Rashmi responded quickly.

'Exactly. If I hadn't enjoyed the journey, I would have given up long before I reached the destination,' Siddharth said. 'What else can we learn?'

'We need to prepare well, and it would be helpful to get advice from an expert so that we don't end up doing the wrong things,' added Naveen.

'Right. I wish I had worked with a trainer or was part of a running group. Instead, I just did all the research on my own without understanding some of the implications. So, working with an expert is definitely advisable,' Siddharth agreed.

'We should expect and face challenges along our journey,' Rajiv said. 'And, to do so, not only should we have a well-thought-out strategy but we should also be flexible to adapt as the terrain and situation change.'

'Excellent,' said Siddharth. 'I couldn't have put it in a better way. That was what enabled me to overcome the issues due to which my race could have ended even before it started.'

'Also, we should be clear that we are not competing with anyone,' Milind added. 'We need to run at our own pace, as our only aim is to enjoy the journey till we reach our destination.'

'Yes, that's the most important thing,' Siddharth emphasized. 'Each one of us is running our own race. There is no point in comparing ourselves with anyone or competing with anyone. With this mindset, even if we get off to a bad start, we can still overcome all hurdles and finish the marathon successfully.'

'As you may have guessed, the marathon is a good analogy for our journey to achieve financial independence,' Siddharth continued. 'First and foremost, as long as we approach it with a positive mindset, enjoy the process, and do not get obsessed with just reaching our goal faster than everyone else, we are sure to achieve it.

'Second, preparation is everything and it would be beneficial to seek the services of an expert in the form of a financial adviser so that we don't make basic mistakes and end up with a mishap that spoils our journey.

'Third, we should have a well-crafted long-term strategy, but at the same time, we should be flexible to adapt to changing circumstances. Here, guidance from a financial adviser can be invaluable, as typically, we are prone to various behavioural biases because of which we might end up taking the wrong decisions.

'The last and most important point to keep in mind is that we are not competing with anyone else. Let's not equate this to amassing the maximum amount of wealth in the minimum amount of time, as it would lead to unhealthy competition and make our journey unpleasant.'

'These are very important learnings, Siddharth,' Mihir said. 'Thanks for sharing them with us in such a lucid manner.'

'Sure. Also, one more thing I have realized is that there is no point in spending a great deal of time tracking each and every expense and investment or getting down to the level of penny-pinching. Everything can't be just about money. Delayed gratification is a good principle but not at the cost of squeezing every little bit out of the present. After all, our lifestyle choices start affecting our family and loved ones too and their support is crucial on this journey. And there's no point trying to look for ways to make money from our hobbies and things we do just for pleasure.'

'So, what is the solution? How do we strike the balance?'

'As I said earlier, let's see financial independence more as a journey rather than a destination. A journey is as much about the present as about our future goals, which can be anything. In fact, the more we enjoy the journey, the greater the chances that we will attain our goal. And the thing about a future goal is that we may or may not always achieve it. But in any case, the journey would still be worthwhile if we enjoyed it rather than it being drudgery.

'To sum it up, financial independence is not some mathematical equation that we solve mechanically. It's a mindset that we need to develop. It's a way of life.'

'Wow, Siddharth, this was a very insightful session,' Kunal said finally. 'I don't think anyone among us thought of financial independence in this way. I wish we had organized this session earlier.'

'Guys, I am glad you found this session helpful,' Siddharth said, 'I have gained these insights over time and am happy to share them with you. Hope we will all apply these principles to our lives.'

'Siddharth, what you have told us today about achieving financial independence makes sense,' everyone agreed. 'But, how do we get down to it?'

'That's where the financial planning part comes in. It's not difficult. The key is to get started and, if we are disciplined, we can tap-dance our way to financial independence. Let me explain with an example,' said Siddharth. 'One of my clients, whom I will call Mr X, has a job at a manufacturing company and his wife, Mrs X, also works in an IT firm. They have two kids. Just after they got married, they had the foresight to plan for the future and came to meet me.

'After understanding their background and goals, we put together a plan wherein they started saving some funds every month and started making regular investments through systematic investment plans in mutual funds. That way, not only did they get exposure to various asset classes like domestic and international stocks, debt, gold, etc., but they could continue to focus on their jobs and raising their kids without having to worry about the financial markets. After a few years, they had built up a sufficient corpus to make a down payment for buying a flat.

'As their income grew over the years, they managed to save more and invested that amount too. And let me tell you, because they have been so disciplined over the past fifteen years, they are living a stress-free life. They are well on their way to attaining specific goals they had set, such as their children's education and marriage, and their own retirement. In fact, their portfolio has done so well that they were even able to go on an international vacation last year. They are really tap-dancing their way to financial independence,' Siddharth explained.

'That's great, Siddharth. But what if I want to invest in stocks directly? Can I do that?' asked Naveen.

'Yes. Even Mr X had expressed some interest in them too. But I convinced him to keep direct stocks separate from his core portfolio. We agreed that he would do it separately with a limited amount which would not be more than 5–10 per cent of his overall portfolio.

'Also, there's all this talk about Bitcoin and non-fungible tokens or NFTs. Do your clients invest in them too? I read that many people have made big money and at the same time many others have lost their shirts too,' Akhil inquired.

'Ha ha. That's true. Some of my clients had asked me about it. But I had advised them to stay away from it as there was rampant speculation going on. For clients who insisted on trying their hand at it, I suggested that they take very limited exposure, not more than 2–3 per cent of their overall portfolio.

'Okay. All of us need to understand all these aspects from you in more detail, Siddharth. Why don't we organize a separate session with you at a later date?' Akhil suggested.

'Sure. I am happy to do it,' Siddharth promised, as they ended the discussion.

Takeaways

1. We should think of achieving financial independence not as a goal but as a marathon journey that we need to enjoy. To finish a marathon, we have to train and prepare well, and enjoy the run. If we don't enjoy the run, we have no chance of finishing.
2. We have to expect and face challenges along the way, and not only follow a clear strategy but also be flexible and adapt to the circumstances.
3. We are not competing with others but need to run at our own pace, as our only aim is to enjoy this marathon journey and cross the finish line.
4. Preparation is everything for this journey and it would be beneficial to seek the services of an expert in the form of a financial adviser, so that we don't make basic mistakes and end up with a mishap that spoils our journey.
5. If done right and with discipline, we can tap-dance our way to financial independence.

CHAPTER 3

Bridging the Trust Gap

The Trust Gap—I Don't Trust Anyone with My Finances

A few days after the reunion, Siddharth was driving back home from his office and was lost in thought.

Over the past decade, he had built up his reputation as a dedicated financial adviser and wealth manager, with offices in Mumbai and Pune. He served clients not only throughout India but also non-resident Indians based in the US, Europe, Middle East and Asia.

He had thousands of interactions with people across all strata of society over the years. The discussions he had were playing on his mind.

'Most of the people coming to me for advice are well-educated and doing reasonably well in their respective fields,' he thought to himself. 'However, when it comes to financial planning and investments, they are behind the curve, almost at a loss regarding what to do. And many lose their way and never really become financially independent, wherein they no longer need to work and can work only if they wish to, or else pursue any other activity that gives them happiness. This also means that they don't achieve their true potential in life or attain their life goals.' Siddharth wondered what was missing and how he could help them more effectively.

Siddharth lived in a high-rise complex in Andheri with his wife, daughter and parents. As he reached home and rang the doorbell, his wife, Shraddha, opened the door.

'Thank God you came home a bit early today,' she said with a sigh of relief. 'Amayra needs some help with her maths homework and is raising hell about it!'

Amayra was their fourteen-year-old daughter. In standard nine itself, her life had become more stressful than Siddharth's.

'Just tell her to calm down. I'll freshen up and help her with it,' Siddharth said.

As he had his tea, Siddharth helped Amayra with a few maths problems. The topic was quadratic equations.

'You know, I used to enjoy solving these problems during my school days,' he said.

'Oh, it seems so simple when you explain it, dad. Not sure why I didn't think of this!' Amayra said as she closed her books. 'I always find maths very easy when you are sitting with me and impossible when you are not around,' she said.

'Dad, you know you have a special gift,' Amayra said fondly as she hugged him.

'Oh, really? And what is that?'

'You can simplify the most complicated thing and explain it in a way that anyone can understand.'

'Thanks, *beta*, you've made my day!' Siddharth smiled.

After some time, he got back to his work, opened his laptop and searched for some data. Finally, he found the information he was looking for, which showed the overall asset allocation of households in India as of March 2022.

Household Asset Allocation in India:

Property: 49.4 per cent
Bank Deposits: 15.1 per cent
Gold: 15.0 per cent
Insurance: 6.2 per cent
Public Provident Fund: 5.7 per cent
Equities: 4.8 per cent
Cash: 3.5 per cent

Of the total household assets in India, 15 per cent was still in bank FDs while investment in equities was less than 5 per cent. And the general population seemed to favour investing in property and gold too.

As he stepped out on to the balcony to get some fresh air, he knew he didn't have to look far for the reasons for such a skewed asset allocation. He settled down in his favourite armchair and thought about his own family.

His wife, Shraddha, was an independent woman and worked as a freelance reporter with a news network. Since their marriage, eighteen years ago, she had preferred to keep her bank account separate and manage her finances independently. She was very diligent about saving her hard-earned money. Unfortunately, she had continued to keep her savings only in FDs and occasionally bought some gold jewellery.

One day she overheard Siddharth explaining to a client over the phone regarding inflation, how FD returns after tax would not beat inflation and hence, why it was not a good idea to keep all of one's savings in FDs.

'Is that so?' she asked him after his call.

'Yes. That's correct,' he answered.

'I don't know about inflation and all that. I just don't trust anyone regarding my money,' she said, 'I am not comfortable keeping my money in anything other than FDs. That's the only thing that gives me peace of mind.'

'I understand that. And believe me, you are not the only one in that camp,' he answered, 'In fact, most people are like you. But you need to know that your money has been losing its value all these years. It's not good at all that you are okay with your savings losing their purchasing power, but you can rationalize it by thinking that it's a hefty fee you are paying to the bank for your peace of mind.'

Siddharth always broke into a smile whenever he remembered this episode and the irony in it. He was one of the well-known financial advisers in the country and his own wife was keeping her money only in FDs and gold!

'Tell me something,' he asked Shraddha. 'You have been keeping your money in FDs only all these years. Can you say that all your savings over the past eighteen years have got you to a position where you don't need to work, and you can just do what makes you truly happy?'

'What does that mean?' Shraddha asked him.

'That's when I would say you are truly financially independent. Are you?'

'No. Far from that. If I was financially independent, I would stop my freelancing work in a jiffy. You know how much I like acting in plays. I used to do that in my college days, and it would give me a lot of joy. And now I only do it occasionally during our annual community gathering. I would love to do that full-time. But if you are now going to tell me to break my FDs and invest in the stock market, I am not going to do that!'

'Why is that?'

'I already told you earlier. I don't trust anyone with my money.'

'The reason most people are not able to successfully complete the journey to financial independence is not just the lack of financial knowledge. The real issue is a lack of trust!' Siddharth told himself.

He also remembered that his father, too, would not discuss his finances with anyone. 'I don't need to tell anyone how much I am earning or how I spend my money. I am quite capable of managing my money and don't trust anyone regarding my finances,' he would say and then go and buy lottery tickets! Siddharth broke into a smile at that thought. 'And he is part of the population that has sunk most of its savings into real estate,' he thought of the flat his father had bought in Pune as an investment.

His father had worked all his life in a government job, and having seen his frustration over the years, Siddharth knew that he could not claim to be financially independent.

'Dad, what would you have done if you were financially independent; I mean, if money was not an issue, and you didn't need to work?' Siddharth asked his father.

'You know how much I love to travel. I would have taken your mom on a long world tour. There are so many places we would have loved to visit. But we were never in a position where we could do that,' he replied wistfully.

'Do you think you could have planned your finances in a better way?' Siddharth prodded him.

'Not sure. But, I did buy lottery tickets to try my luck,' his father replied with a laugh and Siddharth didn't want to push him further.

But he knew the problem was not just with his father alone. Most people preferred to keep their finances to themselves as they were overconfident in their own abilities and didn't trust anyone. They would not ask for help even if they didn't really know much about what options were available to invest their money. In the worst case, they ended up being gullible and losing their hard-earned money by putting it into various schemes and scams. No wonder they never became financially independent.

At that time, Siddharth got a call from his friend Alok who worked at a reputed wealth management firm.

'Tell me something, Alok,' Siddharth said, after chatting for some time. 'You have been in the wealth management business for a long time now and deal with high-net-worth individuals (HNIs) all the time. They are already financially independent, right? What's the biggest issue you face when you deal with them?'

There was a bit of a pause at the other end. 'You know, Siddharth, the biggest issue is lack of trust,' Alok said, after some thought. 'Most of my time just goes in firefighting and answering questions from my clients regarding something I have done or not done.'

'But why is that? As HNIs, their financial knowledge must be higher than the average person's, correct? So, it would be easier for them to understand what you are doing, isn't it?'

'You would think so. But that's really not the case. They are extremely knowledgeable about what they do in their jobs or in the businesses that they run. But that doesn't mean that they are competent in terms of managing their finances.

'On top of that, because they are HNIs, they are solicited by many wealth managers, financial advisers and consultants. So, they get all kinds of inputs. And they may also read various things in newspapers or on the Internet and they come up with their own ideas.

'In the end, all that comes back to me as to why I made a particular investment and not something else.

'I tell you, it can be very frustrating. I wish they would just trust me a bit more. I am sure I can do a lot better if they just let me do my job,' he ended in a weary tone.

'Oh, is that so? I never imagined that would be the case. I used to think you spend all your time wining and dining your high-profile clients and not having to sweat the details,' Siddharth pulled Alok's leg.

'Ha. That happens only in movies. I'd be happy to exchange places with you, if you'd like,' Alok retorted as they ended the call.

'Well, whether it's your family, or the general population, or even the HNIs, the real issue is not just the lack of financial knowledge or overconfidence in one's abilities to manage money. The real issue is the lack of trust!' he told himself again with some satisfaction of having reached the root of the problem.

'Dinner's ready,' Shraddha called out to him.

'Great. I am famished,' he said as he got up from his armchair and headed to the dining table to have dinner with his family.

Ikigai—Do What You Love

Siddharth continued to think about the issue at hand after dinner and his mind was still restless till he finally fell asleep that night.

Surprisingly, when he woke up the next morning, he felt fresh and clear-headed. He liked to start his day early in the morning with an hour of meditation, followed by yoga or a run in the park on alternate days.

As he sat to meditate that day, a lot of thoughts came to his mind and went away. It always happened in the first few minutes. But after that, his mind settled down and he felt calm as all thoughts vanished. His mind went blank, and he concentrated only on his breath.

But today was different. His mind was completely focused on the question of how to bridge the trust gap and increase financial awareness among people.

Finally, he heard his inner voice.

'The Buddha has taught only one thing—the source of human sorrow and how to avoid some of it. Desire and attachment are the root cause of all suffering. Overcoming one's desires and becoming detached leads to happiness.

'I need to follow the same approach. I need to teach people only one thing—the source of financial misery and how they can avoid some of it. If I can help them figure out what doesn't work and then assist them in avoiding or overcoming it, that should help to bridge the trust gap. And if I am able to do that, I can then motivate them on their journey to financial independence and achieving their broader life goals.'

As he wrapped up his meditation session, he felt serene.

'This must be what the Buddha must have experienced too,' he thought to himself with a deep sense of satisfaction. All through the day, he was thinking about the next step.

He remembered that Charlie Munger, Warren Buffet's partner and one of the finest thinkers in the world, had said 'If you figure out what doesn't work in investments and in life and then avoid it, you'll be ahead of 99 per cent of the crowd. Make mistakes but make small mistakes which will not sink you.'

'What that means is one should first think of what may not work and avoid it before getting excited about what may work. In terms of investments, that would mean thinking of risk before returns. Most people think of investments just in terms of returns and that's apparent in their behaviour. They invest their hard-earned money without a proper understanding of the risks involved. And when the returns are not as per their expectations, they get disappointed and spread the word that investing doesn't work. And that leads to a general lack of trust. To break this cycle, I will need to convince them to think of the risks involved in any investment before getting excited about the returns,' Siddharth told himself.

But he knew that it was easier said than done. He knew there was enough literature available on this subject and some financial advisers would have even tried to educate investors in this regard. But nothing seemed to have succeeded so far.

'The issue may be that things are still not presented to investors in a simplified way that they can understand. The data is showing that the investment management industry is still not talking in a language that common people can understand and appreciate,' he thought to himself.

At that moment, he remembered what his daughter, Amayra, had told him the previous day. 'Dad, you have a special gift. You can simplify the most complicated thing and explain it in a way that anyone can understand.'

'Hmm, if there is anyone who can do this, it will be me,' Siddharth said to himself.

Some time ago, he had read a book called *Ikigai*, which talked about finding one's reason for living. 'What is your reason for getting up every morning?' it had asked.

'My mission will be to guide as many people as I can on the right investment path towards financial independence. I will bridge the trust gap by explaining to them in a simple manner the concept of always putting risk before return. That will be my ikigai,' Siddharth said to himself with a sense of satisfaction. He felt energized and looked forward to the next day.

Takeaways

1. The reason most people are not able to successfully complete the journey to financial independence is not just the lack of financial knowledge or overconfidence in their own ability to manage money. The real issue is the lack of trust.
2. We need to understand the source of financial misery and how we can avoid some of it. If we figure out what doesn't work and then avoid or overcome it, it will help us on our journey to financial independence and enable us to achieve our broader life goals.

CHAPTER 4

Risk before Return

The next day, at his meeting with a new client, John Salgaonkar, Siddharth used his new strategy. After understanding John's background, financial situation and goals, he explained the concept of financial independence and how it was akin to undertaking a marathon journey.

'This makes sense, Siddharth,' John said. 'I don't run marathons but would be happy to undertake this journey to financial independence with your guidance.'

'Okay, that's great. But first things first. Before talking of financial independence, it is important to understand that mitigation of real-life risks is the foundation on which the strength to survive any marathon journey can be built.'

'What exactly do you mean by that?'

'I mean that it is important to bear in mind that our life, health and family come first before our finances.

So we need to be adequately insured against loss of life, loss of health and loss of any assets, such as our home. Otherwise, everything can just crumble in an instant and there may not even be a marathon of financial independence to run.'

'Yes, of course. Thanks for reiterating that,' John replied. 'I need to get that in order and will do that right away after our meeting.'

'Okay then, let me ask you a question to start with. As an investor, you can invest in various asset classes such as FDs, stocks, bonds, gold, real estate, currencies, commodities, etc. Which asset class would you choose and why?'

'I guess I would look at their returns for the past one or two years and decide based on that,' John replied along expected lines.

'That's how most people think. But that's not the right way to look at it. Actually, the starting point is to look at their risk–reward profiles, and note that we should put risk before reward,' replied Siddharth, as he showed John some data regarding annual returns of various asset classes. 'As we can see, returns from various asset classes are varying wildly from one year to the next. One year the Indian stock market may do well, the next year, gold or bonds may outperform it, and the next year, maybe international equities may give the best returns. And there is every chance that any of these asset classes may not do well in any given year and you may lose some of your invested capital.'

'Oh, I didn't realize that the returns vary so wildly!'

'Yes, unfortunately, they do. And this is what we mean by risk. So, for example, if you invest in stocks or gold without knowing this underlying variability, you may not be able to beat the FD returns or in the worst case, you may have to face losses in some years.'

'But, with all the data and analytics capabilities we have now, can't we predict the performance of these asset classes?'

'Many people try that. However, predicting the performance of asset classes from one year to the next has become difficult as market cycles, which used to be seven or eight years earlier, have shrunk to three to four years now. Historical correlations between different asset classes, such as the negative correlation between equity and debt, have also become diluted.'

'Oh, and I was going to just look at the past one to two-year returns and make my choice,' John said sheepishly.

'Yes, the worst part is that investors tend to invest based largely on past performance. But if you invest in stocks just because the returns in the past year were good, you may be disappointed. Similarly, if you invest in gold just by looking at the good returns over the past year, it may not happen again.

'Remember that risk is the probability or chance that you may lose some or all of your capital. And you should always bear in mind that you are taking on some risk when you invest in any of these asset classes. Always remember to first look at risk before getting excited about expected returns! Is that understood?'

'Yes. I get it now, Siddharth. I had not put much thought into this. But now I understand the risk I am taking. Thanks for explaining it to me so patiently.'

'Great. Now that we have understood the risk aspect first, let's look at some more data on returns next,' Siddharth said with some relief.

Investment Returns—Things Are Not Always What They Seem

'Since the annual returns vary wildly, we'll look at average returns over a longer period and across periods. This is called the CAGR or compound annual growth rate and gives a better idea about the consistency of returns,' Siddharth continued.

'A key point to keep in mind is that the average inflation in India has been between 4 per cent and 5 per cent over five, ten and fifteen-year periods.

'Now let's check the pre-tax returns for different asset classes and see how they have performed.

'Bank FDs have typically given between 6 and 7 per cent return per annum historically and are around 6 per cent now. So, after tax, they may or may not beat inflation,' said Siddharth.

'That's too bad,' said John.

'Fixed income (bonds) is essentially money that you lend to a company, government or other agency. They have typically given returns that are 0.5 to 1 per cent higher than bank FDs. And if held for the long-term, they have tax advantages. So, after tax, they have a better chance of beating inflation. In that sense, they are better than bank FDs.'

'This is good to know. I have never invested in bonds so far.'

'But, I am sure you have invested in your public provident fund (PPF). It has typically given returns that are 1 to 1.5 per cent higher than bank FDs. So that's okay but still not attractive enough and there is a maximum limit of Rs 1.5 lakh for investment.'

'I understand. PPF can't be the solution to my investment needs.'

'Correct. Now let's look at equities. The stock market has given 12 to 15 per cent returns per annum over the long term, which is reasonably good and can easily beat inflation. However, we need to keep in mind that over the short term, returns can be volatile. That's the risk aspect which I had highlighted to you earlier.'

'Thanks. I used to think the stock market only goes up.'

'It does but only over a long period of time. In the short term, there are a lot of zigzags and it can be volatile. So, you need patience to succeed in the stock market. Most people get disheartened if they see losses or low returns in stocks over a short timeframe and exit at the wrong time.'

'Understood. What about gold? My wife has been buying gold occasionally over the past few years.'

'Ha. Welcome to the club. You can tell her that she has made a reasonably good investment. Till a couple of years ago, gold actually hadn't given good returns over the long term and wouldn't have beaten inflation. But, due to the sharp rally in gold prices over the past few years, returns of close to 10 per cent per annum are looking good. You had better tell your wife that this may or may not sustain going forward.'

'I will. I, on the other hand, have invested in property. Let's see how that has performed.'

'Yes, property has been one of the favourite investments in India. But it has actually given returns less than bank FDs over the past decade as prices have been stagnant for a long time now.'

'So, are you telling me that my wife has been a better investor than me?'

'I am sorry, but that clearly is the case.'

'Good that I didn't bring her along. Else I wouldn't hear the end of it!'

'Ha. At this time, most wives are way ahead of their husbands in terms of investment returns. The key point, as you can see, is that individual asset classes may or may not always deliver the desired returns in the timeframe you want.'

'This is an eye-opener,' said John. 'But why is this so?'

'This is because of the variability in the returns from one year to the next, which is the risk we talked about earlier,' replied Siddharth.

'Got it. But then what is the solution?'

'The solution is to have a balanced asset allocation at all times. Asset allocation has a better chance of delivering stable returns due to the negative correlation between asset classes. For example, if you have a diversified portfolio of domestic stocks, international stocks, bonds, gold and real estate or if you just go with mutual funds and ETFs, which cover these asset classes, then even when one of the asset classes gives poor returns, the other asset classes can balance things out as it is rare that all asset classes underperform at the same time.'

'Okay. But how important really is asset allocation in determining returns?'

'It is very important because studies have shown that 80 to 90 per cent of the performance variability between an investor's portfolio and the market is due to the asset allocation and less than 10 to 20 per cent is due to individual asset selection or market timing. What this means is that how your portfolio is divided between equity or stocks, debt or bonds, gold, real estate, FDs, etc., is more important than any single stock, bond or any other asset you may own.'

'Oh, is that so?' said John. 'I didn't know that.'

'Well, most investors don't. And the sad part is that most waste a lot of their time trying to get some stock tips, or invest in some property, etc.'

'Yes, I am guilty of that too,' John said with a bit of embarrassment.

'That's because you can brag about your latest stock picks or property investment with your friends. If you try to talk about asset allocation, most people won't understand or appreciate what you are saying,' Siddharth ended with a smile.

'I was on the wrong track so far and have understood now that I need to have a balanced asset allocation.

Thanks so much, Siddharth, for explaining everything in a language that I could understand.'

'It's my pleasure,' said Siddharth as he saw the first signs of success in following his new strategy.

'Even if I can help a fraction of potential investors on their journey to financial independence, I will be able to impact a large number of lives,' Siddharth thought, pleased with himself. 'That will be my contribution to society.'

Takeaways

1. We need to think of the risks involved in any investment first, before getting excited about the returns.
2. A balanced asset allocation is crucial. 80 to 90 per cent of the performance variability between an investor's portfolio and the market is due to asset allocation and less than 10 to 20 per cent is due to individual product selection or market timing.

CHAPTER 5

Asset Allocation:
The Starting Point

Siddharth was absorbed in reading a report in his office a few days later when he heard a knock on his door.

'The Sharmas are here for their 3 p.m. appointment,' his assistant, Maryann, informed him.

'Sure, please send them in,' he told Maryann.

A middle-aged couple walked into his office hesitatingly.

'Hi, I am Akshara and this is my husband, Vedant Sharma. I attended your seminar last week and after speaking with you, I had booked an appointment.'

'Yes, of course, I remember that. Please take a seat. How can I help you?'

'Let me give you a brief background,' began Vedant. 'I work in sales at a multinational company (MNC) and

Akshara works in the human resources (HR) department of a bank. I am thirty-five and she is thirty-two and we have two children aged six and three. We stay with my parents in our own flat.'

'Okay, please go on,' said Siddharth.

'The issue is, we have always been very haphazard with our finances and don't seem to have any control,' Vedant continued. 'Our parents are getting old, our children are growing up fast, and we are busy running on the corporate treadmill. We have never really sat down and made a plan for the future.'

'So, after attending your seminar, I spoke to Vedant and we thought it would be a good idea for us to seek your services as a financial adviser,' Akshara added.

'Sure, I'll be happy to do that,' said Siddharth. 'Let's make sure we understand the big picture first before we get into the details,' he added.

'Every investor is actually on a journey to financial independence, whether they realize it or not,' Siddharth told them as he explained the concept. 'And what they should aim for is to complete this journey joyfully and easily, instead of getting stressed about it. That's why I like to call it tap-dancing to financial independence.'

'You are right. We are absolutely stressed right now, and we would really like you to show us how this can be easy and give us some joy. We'd like to tap-dance, as you put it.'

'Great. I am glad you understood this,' Siddharth continued, 'The starting point for any investor is asset allocation. As an investor, you can invest in various asset classes such as savings accounts and FDs, stocks (domestic, international, emerging markets, etc.), bonds (corporate, government, high-yield, etc.), gold, real estate, currencies (or forex), commodities, etc.'

'Yes, we have invested in some of them.'

'Well, each of them has a different risk-reward profile. Asset allocation essentially looks at how you should balance your investment across various asset classes in your portfolio. It increases the chances of getting your desired return along with optimal exposure to the underlying risk factors.'

'Oh, that's a bit too technical for us. Can you explain it in simple terms?'

'Sure, let me explain with an analogy. I am sure you tell your children that they should have a proper meal consisting of roti, sabji, rice, dal, salad, dessert, etc., rather than just hogging on junk food. Is that correct?'

'Yes, absolutely.'

'Why do you do that?'

'So that they get all the necessary nutrients such as proteins, carbohydrates, fats and vitamins.'

'Exactly. And for them to get the nutrients in the right proportion, the meal must be balanced, right? Else, if they just eat the dessert because they like it but not the salad, it's not going to have the best result, correct?'

'Absolutely. We try our best to ensure they have a balanced meal. That's best for their health.'

'Similarly, if you keep your savings only in your savings account and in FDs, it's like eating just salads all the time. You may think it is healthy because it is low-risk, but you will not get all the necessary nutrients. At the same time, putting your money only in stocks is like eating just dessert all the time. You may enjoy it because it gives you an immediate kick, but it is high-risk and likely to lead to diabetes down the line.'

'Oh, we never thought of it like that.'

'That's why we recommend that investors should have a balanced portfolio across equity, that is, domestic and international stocks), fixed income or debt, which are corporate and government bonds), gold, real estate, etc., so that they get stable returns while reducing the overall portfolio risk. So, for example, a balanced asset allocation can look as follows:

Domestic equity: 60 per cent

International equity: 6 per cent

Gold: 10 per cent

Fixed income: 24 per cent

'In addition, some investors would also have some real estate which they may have bought for investment purposes but let's ignore that for the moment.'

'But how does asset allocation reduce the risk while giving stable returns?'

'That happens because these asset classes are negatively correlated.'

'What does that mean?'

'That means that if one asset class like stocks underperforms at some point in time, other asset classes like gold or bonds are likely to outperform it and balance things out. That's how asset allocation helps your portfolio remain healthy over the long term.'

'We understand now. But is this a one-time thing where we decide the allocation once and forget about it?'

'No. It's an ongoing process. We need to monitor the portfolio and track the returns on our investments. And we need to rebalance the portfolio at regular intervals, say every 3–6 months, so that it is suitable for the market conditions. For example, let's say we start with an allocation that looks like this:

Equity: 60 per cent

Debt: 30 per cent

Gold: 10 per cent

'And then the stock market rallies over the next six months. The weight of the equity asset class in our portfolio may increase and our allocation may have changed as follows:

Equity: 65 per cent

Debt: 28 per cent

Gold: 7 per cent

Then we would need to decide whether to rebalance our portfolio and reduce our equity allocation back to 60 per cent while increasing the allocation to debt and gold.'

'This is clear now. Asset allocation is a process we need to follow. Understood,' Vedant said after some thought.

'Yes. It was very nice of you to explain it to us in a simple manner so that we could understand,' Akshara said.

'Okay, you mentioned that you have invested in some of these asset classes.'

'Yes. We've brought the documents with us.'

'Great. I'll go through them. And in our next meeting, let's look at your asset allocation and see how balanced it is. That will give us a pulse of the health of your portfolio.'

'Sure. And after that, what would be the next steps?'

'You'll start by learning a new framework that covers five basic principles of financial planning.'

'That sounds exciting. We can't wait to hear more about it.'

'We'll discuss it the next time we meet,' Siddharth ended the meeting with a smile.

Keep Your Insurance and Investments Separate

The next day, Shefali and Abhay Maheshwari came to meet Siddharth at his office. Abhay worked at a reputed car manufacturer while Shefali was a homemaker. They had a three-year-old son.

'Our bank's relationship manager has been calling me for the past few days to talk about an insurance-cum-investment product or unit linked insurance plan or ULIP as he called it,' Abhay said. 'He said it would be ideal for me as it provides the safety of insurance as well as good returns, along with a tax deduction. I didn't fully understand it. So, I thought it was best to discuss it with you before he calls me again. He is very persistent.'

'I see. Let me ask you a couple of questions first. Why do you buy insurance?' Siddharth asked Abhay.

'So that if something happens to me, my family will not have to face financial problems.'

'Correct. And why do you invest?'

'So that my savings are protected from inflation and it can give me an opportunity for wealth creation.'

'Excellent. So clearly, these are two different objectives, correct?'

'Yes. Absolutely.'

'In that case, doesn't it make sense to keep your insurance and investment separate so that you can buy the best insurance product for yourself and separately ensure that you have the right asset allocation on the investment side?'

'Yes. That makes sense. But, what goes wrong when we combine them?'

'If you combine the two, like in a ULIP, you may not get the best product to meet either your insurance goals or your investment goals. Your insurance cover will likely be too small to make any difference to your family and the returns are likely to disappoint you.'

'Oh. I understand now,' Abhay said. 'But why did my bank's relationship manager say that the ULIP was an ideal product for me?'

'Well, it is an ideal product, but for him and not for you. The bank and their RMs get a higher fee for selling a ULIP than for most other products. So, they are incentivized to push them to customers like you.'

'Is that so? I didn't know that,' Abhay exclaimed.

'See. I told you it was best to check with Siddharth on this,' Shefali nudged Abhay.

'I am glad you came to discuss this with me. The key thing to understand is that we should always separate insurance and investments. We have talked about investments before. Let's talk about insurance now. There are various types like life insurance, health insurance and others like vehicle insurance, home insurance, accident and disability insurance, etc.

Life Insurance

'Life insurance is chiefly a risk management tool meant to offer financial protection to your dependents in the unfortunate event of your death. If you are adequately insured, your life insurance should enable your dependents—spouse, children and parents—to maintain their current lifestyle and pursue their financial goals until the time they are able to set up an alternate income stream on their own.'

'How much should my insurance cover be?'

'A rule of thumb is that your life insurance should be eight to ten times your annual take-home income. Think of it as the money your family can put in an FD or mutual fund or tax-free bond to generate a regular income.'

'I know that there are various types of life insurance policies available and it's very confusing. Which one should we go for?'

'Remember that the only objective of life insurance is protection. Some life insurance policies offer investment options or some other features, but I wouldn't recommend that you go with them. The best option is to go with a term plan, which is a no-frills policy in which the nominee gets the sum assured if the policyholder dies during the tenure of the policy. Of course, nothing accrues if the policyholder outlives the term of the policy, but this is a bet that everyone should aspire to lose.'

'Is this the right time for me to buy insurance?'

'It is best to buy life insurance when one is relatively young and healthy, just as you are now, so that you don't have to pay high premiums later.'

'Should I go through an agent or can I buy this policy online?'

'Nowadays, you can buy policies online to save intermediary costs and get a higher cover for lower premium amounts.'

'Is there a tax benefit to buying a life insurance policy?'

'Yes. Premiums paid towards a life insurance policy qualify for tax deductions under Section 80C with a limit of Rs 1.5 lakh in a financial year.

'Let's also look at another type of insurance that you should seriously consider, which is health insurance.'

Health Insurance

'As you both are aware, we are facing rising healthcare costs and growing lifestyle diseases. In this scenario, health insurance is a vital financial tool to address our healthcare needs.'

'How does it work?'

'Health insurance works as a financial protection tool against medical expenses. It usually provides either direct payment or reimbursement for expenses associated with illness, injury and hospitalization. The cost and range of protection provided by a health insurance policy depend on the insurer and the type of policy. Some policies also cover pre- and post-hospitalization expenses. Most policies have to be renewed annually.'

'I am already enrolled in the group health plan of my company. Isn't that enough?'

'It's good since it would come with certain additional benefits, such as pregnancy cover or covering pre-existing conditions, etc. But since it is backed by your employer, it is good only as long as you stay with your employer.

'However, you should not depend just on this cover. I would recommend that you augment it with an additional separate insurance cover of your own. You never know when you would need it.'

'Okay. What type of policy cover would we need to buy?'

'Well, a single individual can go for an individual health plan and if one is young, they do not need to buy a very high cover as their health is likely to remain good. They can add more cover with increasing age.

'However, for a family like yours, it is recommended to go for a family-floater plan wherein the policy covers the family members, for example, two adults and two children.

'Also keep in mind that health insurance policies are portable, which means that one can move from one insurer to another by transferring their existing policies to a new insurer.'

'Do these give any tax benefits?'

'Yes. Tax premiums paid towards health insurance are tax deductible under Section 80(D) of the Income Tax Act.'

'Great. Thanks, Siddharth. This was a real eye-opener for us. I am glad we came and met you. We will get our insurance sorted out at the earliest.' Abhay and Shefali let out a sigh of relief.

'Excellent. And remember to always keep your insurance and investments separate,' Siddharth ended with a smile.

Takeaways

1. The starting point for any investor is asset allocation.
2. Asset allocation looks at how we should balance our investments across various asset classes in our portfolio. It increases the chances of getting our desired return along with optimal exposure to the underlying risk factors.
3. Investors should have a balanced portfolio across domestic and international stocks, corporate and government bonds, gold, real estate, etc., so that they get stable returns while reducing the overall portfolio risk.
4. Asset allocation works because of the negative correlation between asset classes. That means that if one asset class, such as stocks, underperforms at some point in time, other asset classes like gold or bonds are likely to outperform it and balance things

out. That's how asset allocation helps our portfolio to remain healthy over the long term.

5. We should always keep our insurance and investments separate. For life insurance, the best option is to go with a term plan.

6. We should augment the health insurance cover we get through our employer with an additional separate insurance cover of our own.

CHAPTER 6

Savings before Expenses: The First Principle of Financial Planning

Siddharth had wrapped up his work for the day. He was about to leave his office and head home when his phone rang. It was his nephew, Karan.

'Hi *mamu*, how are you? Hope I didn't catch you at a bad time,' Karan said.

'No. Not at all,' said Siddharth as he settled back in the ergonomic chair in his office. 'What's up?' he asked.

'Well, as you know, I just graduated and am going to start my job at a fintech start-up in Bengaluru.'

'Yes, of course.'

'So, mom asked me to speak to you so that I can get started right in terms of managing my finances.'

Siddharth had a long roster of clients for his financial advisory service and also advised his family, friends and relatives. He was pleased. 'You know, I am impressed that you are already thinking in the right direction,' he said.

'Thanks, mamu. But you know that's what I always do, right?' said Karan.

'Not always, but sometimes, yes, I would agree.' Siddharth replied with a smile to himself remembering Karan's mischievousness.

'So, what am I supposed to do?' asked Karan.

'Well, you studied mathematics, didn't you?'

'Yes. I did.'

'Then, I am sure you know about the relation between your income, expenses and savings, right?'

'Yes. That's easy. My income minus my expenses will equal my savings,' said Karan with confidence.

Income – Expenses = Savings

'Well, that's what they teach you in school,' replied Siddharth. 'But do you also know Carl Jacobi?'

'No, I don't.'

'He was a famous mathematician. And his principle was "Invert. Always invert."'

'So, if you want to get to the right answer, then learn to think about a problem both forwards and backwards. In this case, what would you get if you invert whatever you have learnt traditionally about income, expenses and savings?'

'Well, it would be my income minus my savings will equal my expenses,' exclaimed Karan.

Income – Savings = Expenses

'You are absolutely right, congratulations,' said Siddharth, pleased with Karan and with himself. 'That is the first principle of financial planning.

'Make sure that when you receive your salary, you first set aside at least 10 to 20 per cent as your savings and spend only the remaining amount.

'And, remember Benjamin Franklin's maxim: 'Beware of little expenses; a small leak will sink a great ship.' All your small discretionary or impulse spending will add up,' Siddharth continued.

'But, this is my first job. Do you think the salary I will receive will be sufficient for me to save anything, especially in a city like Bengaluru?' asked Karan incredulously.

'That's the whole point. Always keep the first principle in mind and prepare your budget accordingly. Remember that your savings come before your expenses.'

'And where should I keep my savings?'

'Oh, that's easy. You should open a savings account with a large, established bank. Your money will be safe, you will get moderate interest on that, and you can also withdraw your money whenever you need it.

'Also, you will get a chequebook and an ATM card as well as Internet banking and mobile banking facilities.'

'That's great. I always wanted my own ATM card,' said Karan. 'I am glad I spoke to you, mamu,' he continued. 'I will keep the first principle in mind.'

'Good. I am happy that you called me and that I could be of help. All the best,' said Siddharth as he put the phone down and took a deep breath. He was glad that Karan would be taking the right first step in his lifelong financial journey.

As he drove home that evening, he felt a sense of satisfaction. He knew how important taking the right first step was in any journey.

Takeaways

1. Income – Savings = Expenses.
2. When we receive our salary, we should first set aside at least 10 to 20 per cent as our savings and spend only the remaining amount.
3. Beware of the little expenses. All our small discretionary or impulse spending adds up.

7

Compound Interest— The Most Powerful Force: The Second Principle of Financial Planning

'Karan, how are you doing it?' his friend Dishant asked him. 'How are you able to save some money from your paycheck while we aren't?'

Karan had joined his job at a fintech start-up in Bengaluru. He lived with three of his friends—Ajay, Mihir and Dishant—in a flat in Koramangala. It had been six months and he had adjusted to life there. On a Friday night, Karan and his flatmates had come to M.G. Road to hang out. They had decided to have pizza at Domino's.

'I even had to ask my dad to send me some money,' continued Mihir. 'The money we make is not enough to live in this city.'

'Agreed. We need to be enjoying ourselves at this stage of our life,' said Ajay. 'And here we are, sitting with near-empty wallets.'

They all turned to Karan for an answer. He was the only one among them who seemed to be living comfortably and was also able to save some money every month.

'It's very simple, *yaar*. I am just following the first principle of financial planning,' said Karan as he picked up a slice of the Mexican green wave pizza.

'What is that? I've never heard of it,' Ajay said while digging into his double cheese Margherita pizza.

'Income − Savings = Expenses,' Karan said with a smile.

'Hold on. Shouldn't it be Income − Expenses = Savings?' asked Mihir.

'No. You heard right. It's based on the concept of inversion by Carl Jacobi, a famous mathematician,' Karan said confidently. 'The first principle says that your income minus your savings should be your expenses. That's why I target to save 10 to 20 per cent of my in-hand pay and only spend the remaining amount.'

'But I am sure you would be compromising on a lot of things then, right?' asked Ajay.

'Not at all. I am enjoying myself as much as you guys. I have only cut back on any unnecessary excess spending. Knowing that I have a fixed amount to spend helps me control my expenses. Why don't you guys also give it a shot?'

'The first principle, huh?' said Dishant after some thought. 'I am willing to try it.'

'Let me see if you can do it for a month or two and then I'll decide,' said Ajay.

'I'll leave you guys to try it out. I am just going to ask my dad if I run out of money. I am sure he will understand.' Mihir was very clear.

They finished their pizza and went to see a movie.

'Hi mamu,' a familiar voice greeted Siddharth on the phone the next morning.

'Hi Karan, how are you doing?' asked Siddharth, happy to hear his nephew's voice at the other end.

'I am doing great. And I wanted to share some good news with you!' exclaimed Karan. 'I kept the first principle in mind and managed to save 10 to 20 per cent of the salary I got in hand every month.'

'Excellent, Karan, I am proud of you.'

'I had to make a few sacrifices along the way, but I have a sense of accomplishment today. And you know what? None of my friends has managed to save any money! In fact, they are now asking me for tips on what to do.'

'Ha. That's what happens when you work from first principles and others don't.'

'So, what next, mamu? What should I do now?'

'For the next step, you don't have to be Einstein. But you just have to pay heed to what he said.'

'Oh, you mean his famous equation, $E = mc2$? How does that fit in my financial journey?'

'That's what he is famous for. But that's not the only thing. He once said that the most powerful force in the world is compound interest.'

'Oh, is that so? They taught us the compound interest formula in our school but didn't tell us that it was such an important formula to keep in mind.'

'That's the unfortunate part. But that's the second principle of financial planning, namely, one who understands compound interest, receives it. And one who doesn't, pays it. In simple terms, it is interest on interest.'

$$V = P * (1 + r) \wedge t$$

Where

P = initial principal amount invested

r = interest rate

t = time period, the most critical parameter in the equation

V = value the principal amount grows to after time period t

He looked at a sheet of paper on his desk which had a table showing compounding returns. 'Let's see, if we invest Rs 100 at a 10 per cent interest rate, it will double in around seven years. At a 15 per cent interest rate, it will double in five years and at 20 per cent interest rate, in just over three and a half years.'

'Oh, is that so?'

'Yes. And do you know that compound interest is the only formula with a power in the exponent? That's what makes it so powerful. Time is on our side in this formula.'

'Yes. I remember the formula. But where can I get compound interest?'

'Actually, your savings account is already paying you compound interest, but you can do better and get a higher interest rate if you open an FD.'

'I've heard my parents talk about FDs earlier. What are they?'

'FD stands for fixed deposit. In an FD, you deposit your money with the bank for a specified period ranging from fifteen days to ten years at a fixed interest rate, which is typically higher than in a savings account. And because of compounding, you earn better interest and your money grows at a faster rate than in an ordinary savings bank account.'

'Okay. I understand that the main attraction is the higher interest rate along with compounding for the tenure of the FD. But there is no free lunch, right? Are there any drawbacks to an FD?'

'You are smart. Your money is essentially locked in for the tenure of the FD. But if you need the money urgently, you can close the deposit early with a penalty or you can get a loan of 75 to 90 per cent of the deposit at an interest rate slightly higher than the FD rate.'

'That's not too bad. I can live with that if I can get higher compound interest in return.'

'Excellent. I am glad you understood this second principle of financial planning.'

'Thanks, mamu. I will keep only a small amount in my savings account and go ahead and open an FD tomorrow with the rest of my savings.'

Siddharth was pleased as he put the phone down. He wished that more youngsters would show the maturity and understanding that Karan had shown. He had normally seen newly employed graduates spending their salary on eating out and partying, or buying fancy clothes and gadgets and then not being left with any significant savings. He wished he could educate youngsters to think carefully about their first steps on their lifetime financial journey.

Takeaways

1. Compound interest is the most powerful force in the world.
2. One who understands compound interest, receives it. And one who doesn't, pays it.
3. Time is on our side in the compound interest formula.

CHAPTER 8

Emergency Fund: The Third Principle of Financial Planning

'Hi Disha, we are over here,' Simran called out to Disha and pointed to a small group at a table. They were at a pub in Kamala Mills Compound in Mumbai. Every Friday evening, Disha and her friends used to get together at a different pub in the city.

Disha was a twenty-four-year-old journalist. Her friends were all in different professions and they had been together since their college days. Whenever they met, they could talk endlessly on varied topics from movies, sports and office gossip to reminiscing about the past.

'Listen up, everyone. I have some good news to share,' Sameer announced after some time. 'I have made some money in the stock market and I am going to buy a brand-new bike. The next round of drinks is on me. Cheers!'

'Way to go, Sameer,' everyone cheered and patted Sameer on his back. 'You have to give us some tips too.'

'How did you manage to do that, Sameer?' Disha asked him. 'Do you have someone to advise you?'

'I don't need advice, Disha,' Sameer replied. 'Making money in stocks is very easy. By the way, what's the situation with you guys on the money front? If you'd like, I can invest it for you in the stock market.'

'Ha. This is a no-brainer for me. I just spend all my money every month. So, there is nothing to invest,' Simran laughed.

'Me too, I am in the same boat,' a few others joined her.

'What about you, Disha?' asked Sameer.

'Actually, I have a financial adviser,' Disha replied.

'Ooh, you have your own financial adviser. You must be rolling in money,' everyone teased her.

'Which stocks has your financial adviser put your money in?' Sameer asked her. 'I can give you some stock tips if you'd like but you'll have to buy a round of drinks for us next time.'

'Actually, I only managed to start saving some money over the past year based on his advice. But, he has put most of my savings in fixed deposits,' Disha answered.

'FDs,' everyone burst out laughing. 'That's so boring.'

'Isn't that something our parents and grandparents put their money in?' Sameer pointed out to her. 'We are young folks. We can take a lot of risk.'

'Absolutely. If not now, then when?' Simran supported him.

'Why don't you speak to that financial adviser of yours and tell him that I can help you invest in stocks?' Sameer added. 'What's the point of having an adviser if he's putting your money in FDs anyways?'

Disha was lost in thought as she left the get-together that night.

Siddharth was reading a report in his office on Monday morning when Disha walked in. She had been his client for the past year. Before she had met Siddharth through a mutual friend, she didn't know much about financial planning and always used to be under stress about her small bank balance.

But Siddharth had educated her about the first two principles, namely, savings before expenses and compound interest and she had been convinced that this was the right path.

'Hi Siddharth, as you know, based on your guidance I have cut back on my expenses and have also managed to start a few FDs with the money I saved,' Disha started.

'Yes. Congratulations!' said Siddharth.

'Well, I met a few friends last week and some of them were talking about how they had put some money in the stock market, and it had doubled in a few months. When I told them that I had put my money in FDs, they made fun of me. They said that FDs were boring, and we were too young for FDs.'

'That's too bad.'

'My friend, Sameer, especially seems to have done very well. He has made some quick money in stocks which he said will enable him to make the down payment for purchasing a new bike.'

'Good for him.'

'So, I wanted to ask you if I should also put some money in the stock market.'

'Do you even know what the stock market is?'

'No. But I am sure you do, and it seems exciting. Can't you guide me? Else, Sameer said he would be happy to invest the money for me.'

'Let me ask you one question first. Do you have money that you can afford to lose?'

'What do you mean?'

'Basically, if you lose that money, it won't make a difference in your day-to-day life or won't cause you undue stress.'

'Not really. As you know I have just been able to start saving some money and every rupee counts.'

'Well then, this is not the right time for you to think about the stock market or any other investment.'

'So, when will it be the right time to think about these things?'

'For that you need to understand the third principle of financial planning, which is that you should have an emergency fund which will cover six to twelve months of your expenses. And this can be in the form of FDs.'

'Is that really necessary? I don't think anything is going to happen to me.'

'That's why it's called an emergency fund, because emergencies don't inform you before coming. It can be anything from a medical emergency or job loss or some totally unexpected expense. This is for the unknown of unknowns.

'Believe me, quite a few of my clients have been saved from tough times just because they had an emergency fund. And FDs are good in this regard. With just a savings account, you may be tempted to withdraw the money and spend it. But with an FD, you will have to pay a penalty if you want to break your FD, which will force you to think twice.'

'Oh. I understand now. But I am still quite some time away before my savings can cover six to twelve months of my expenses.'

'Don't worry. It won't take that long. And you are young with a long life ahead of you. So, you will have enough time to evaluate the stock market and other investment products. But let's leave that for a later time. For now, your only milestone should be to set up your emergency fund.'

'Okay, Siddharth. What you have told me makes sense. I will follow this third principle of financial planning. Also, it makes sense for me to make my friends aware of the need for an emergency fund. I don't think anyone has thought about it.'

'Excellent, Disha. I am glad you are making the right choice. Good luck,' Siddharth said as Disha got up to leave.

A couple of months later, Disha and her friends got together on a Friday, at a restaurant in Bandra. As usual, they had a good time catching up and talking about myriad topics. However, Sameer was unusually quiet and brooding.

'What's the matter, Sameer?' Simran asked him. 'Are you not well?'

'I am fine,' Sameer replied, although it was clear he was stressed out. 'Actually, I had made a few risky bets in the stock market based on some tips I had received. And I have lost all my money. I have to pay my rent in a few days, and I don't have any savings.'

'Oh. That's too bad, Sameer,' everyone consoled him. 'But don't worry, we'll all chip in so that at least you can cover your rent.'

'Sameer, last month I had told you all about the need for an emergency fund,' Disha added. 'It's in times like this that we all understand its value.'

'Yes, Disha. You are right,' replied Sameer. 'I shouldn't have taken so much risk. I didn't know what I was doing. Could you please take me along when you meet your financial adviser next? I have learnt my lesson and would like to mend my ways.'

'Sure, Sameer. I'd be happy to introduce you to Siddharth. He can show you the right path. I will speak to him tomorrow morning itself and check when we can go and meet him.'

The next morning, Siddharth got a call from Disha. She mentioned how her friend Sameer had lost quite a big chunk of money in the stock market and was visibly stressed out when they had met. Not only had his plans to buy a new bike gone down the drain but all his savings were also wiped out. He would have to start from scratch.

'Thanks, Siddharth.' Disha said over the phone, 'I feel so relieved that I have an adviser like you.'

'Of course, Disha. That's what an adviser is for. To make sure you walk on the right path during your financial journey.'

'Yes. And now even Sameer wants to come and meet you. He has realized his mistake and wants to make amends.'

'Of course, Disha. I'd be happy to guide him too. Take care,' Siddharth said as they ended the call.

Takeaways

1. We should have an emergency fund that will cover six to twelve months of our expenses. And this can be in the form of FDs.
2. We should think of investing in any risky asset only after we have an emergency fund in place.

CHAPTER 9

Market Risk: The Fourth Principle of Financial Planning

'Hi Siddharth, welcome!' Anant said as he opened the door to his rented flat in Mumbai and invited Siddharth inside.

Anant and Hema Pandit had gotten married recently. They had both graduated as engineers and had been working at a leading IT services company for the past four years where they had met each other. Showing some foresight, Hema's elder brother had given them a one-year subscription to Siddharth's financial advisory service as a wedding gift so that they could plan their finances properly.

They broke the ice with some chit-chat over tea and biscuits. Afterwards, when Siddharth reviewed their finances with them, he was happy to see that they had some savings but was also surprised that after four years of being employed, their savings were not significant.

'Oh, that's simple. While we had a modest wedding, we decided to splurge on an international honeymoon. After all, YOLO—you only live once!' they explained together.

'That's only fair,' said Siddharth. 'So, what do you want to do going forward?'

'Well, we discussed this in preparation for our meeting. We both are clear that our priority is to save enough to make a down payment for buying our own flat. But Hema is comfortable keeping our savings in FDs only. While I think, at this stage in our lives, we can take a little more risk and look at other investments,' said Anant.

'Yes. That's right. My parents used to keep their savings in FDs, and I believe FDs are the way to go for us too. Why do we even need to consider anything else?' Hema added.

'Okay. Let's take this step by step,' said Siddharth as he walked them through the first three principles of financial planning, namely, savings before expenses, compound interest and emergency fund.

Fortunately, both Anant and Hema were ahead of the curve on this front.

'We have a monthly budget, manage to save around 15–20 per cent of our in-hand salary, and have savings in FDs that can cover more than a year of our expenses,' they said with some satisfaction.

'Okay. So, the question now is what next?' said Siddharth. 'You are quite clear that you want to make a down payment for buying a flat. But do you have any timeframe in mind?' he asked.

'We both are twenty-six years old. And we would like to buy our own flat in two years before we start a family,' Hema responded with a clarity of mind that impressed Siddharth.

'Yes. We both are on the same page on that,' added Anant.

'Fine. If you are clear on that, then I'd suggest you first decide your budget for buying a new flat. Then we can figure out how much of a loan you can get from a bank and hence, how much of a down payment you would need to make. After that, we can work out the monthly amount you would need to save and put in a bank RD so that at the end of two years, you will be ready with your down payment amount.'

'I have only heard of an FD. What is an RD?' asked Hema.

'RD stands for recurring deposit. Like an FD, an RD is also a product that allows you to earn compound interest. In an RD, you contribute a fixed amount every month for a fixed tenure, which can range from six months to ten years, at an interest rate higher than in a savings account. The difference between an FD and an RD is that the RD will compel you to save a fixed amount every month.'

'I understand. It will give us some discipline. So, we will open an RD with a two-year tenure,' said Anant.

'And, we would have to save a fixed amount and add it to the RD every month,' added Hema.

'Correct. I am glad we got that clear,' Siddharth said.

'But, are there any drawbacks in an RD?' Hema asked.

'Your money is essentially locked in for the tenure of the RD,' Siddharth clarified. 'But if you need the money urgently, you can close the deposit early with a penalty or you can get a loan of 75–90 per cent of the deposit at an interest rate slightly higher than the RD rate.'

'That's fine. Anyway, we have our separate emergency fund and hopefully won't need to break the RD,' said Hema.

'But since we have two years to make our down payment, can't we look at some other investment products like stocks or bonds?' asked Anant.

'You have to understand that in the investment world, two years is a short time horizon,' Siddharth answered. 'And stocks, bonds and other investments are subject to market risk.'

'Now, what does that mean?' Anant raised an eyebrow.

'It means these products can give negative returns at times, that is, it is possible that you could see losses and end up with an amount less than the target amount for your goal after two years. That's what is called market risk,' Siddharth explained.

'But some of our colleagues have invested in stocks and bonds. How come they are doing it?' Anant asked him.

'Simple. Either they don't have a fixed goal with a short timeframe like you,' Siddharth told him, 'or, they may not fully appreciate the risk they are taking and may end up short. In the best case, maybe they know what they are doing and hopefully, their luck favours them.'

'Okay. I understand now,' Anant said.

'Let me put it differently. Do you have money you can afford to lose at this stage?'

'No way! We will be on a tight budget if we are to buy our own flat,' Hema responded quickly.

'Well, that settles it then,' Siddharth said with an air of finality. 'This is the fourth principle of financial planning. Don't invest unnecessarily in investment products subject to market risk if you have a fixed goal with a short time horizon.'

'It's clear to me now. We are not in a position to take market risks at this time,' said Anant.

'Correct. You are not. Warren Buffett, the most famous investor in the world, has laid down two important rules for investments which I would like you to always bear in mind,' Siddharth continued.

'Oh. We've heard of him. What did he say?' asked Anant.

'Well, his rules are:

Rule No. 1: Don't lose money.

Rule No. 2: Don't forget Rule No. 1.'

'Ha ha. That's good. We'll surely keep that in mind,' said Anant.

'Thanks, Siddharth. I am so glad that we met you today. Now I understood why my brother gifted us a year's worth of your advisory services. It's worth its weight in gold,' Hema beamed.

'Yes. I agree, Siddharth. Based on your advice, we are clear now regarding what we need to do,' added Anant.

'That's great. Let's review your progress after three months and make sure you are still on track,' said Siddharth as he got up to leave.

'We will look forward to it,' both Hema and Anant said in unison.

Takeaways

1. Some investment products can give negative returns at times, i.e., it's possible that we could see losses and end up with an amount less than the target amount for our goal. This is called market risk.
2. We should not invest unnecessarily in investment products subject to market risk if we have a fixed goal with a short time horizon.
3. Capital preservation is crucial.

10

The Elephant in the Room—Beating Inflation: The Fifth Principle of Financial Planning

'Hello, friends,' began Siddharth, 'Thanks for coming for today's seminar on financial planning and investments.'

Every month, Siddharth used to hold a free seminar in a mid-sized auditorium of a hotel, alternately in Mumbai and Pune. This time the session was being held in Borivali in Mumbai. There were about 100 people in attendance, and they were across all age groups. To his pleasant surprise, Hema Pandit, who he had met a few days ago, had also come along with her group of ten ladies.

'Let's start with the basics,' he said as he covered the first four principles of financial planning, namely, savings before expenses, compound interest, emergency fund and market risk.

There were a few questions from the audience which he answered to everyone's satisfaction.

'This is not so difficult, right? Can everyone follow these principles?' he asked and got an affirmative response.

'You seem to be extremely happy, sir,' Siddharth pointed to a middle-aged gentleman in the audience. 'I can see you smiling ear-to-ear.'

'Yes,' the man sounded a bit embarrassed with the attention. 'Actually, I seem to have followed all these principles to the T. And I have kept most of my savings in FDs, which are very safe. I have never lost any money,' he said with pride.

A few other audience members also joined him. 'We've also kept all our savings in FDs only. Why take unnecessary risk?'

'That's what I tell my husband. But he just doesn't listen,' one of the ladies in the audience said amid laughter.

'That's very good,' replied Siddharth, 'But now, let's come to the elephant in the room. All of this is necessary but may not be sufficient. And do you know why?' He loved quizzing his audience.

A few hands went up, but nobody could give him the answer he wanted.

'A few minutes ago, I told you that compound interest was the strongest force in the world. And you can channel it to work for you. But there is a similar force that works against you.' He gave them a hint but only saw blank faces.

He then turned to the group of ladies. 'When you go to buy your monthly groceries, over the years, have you seen the prices increasing or decreasing?'

'Always increasing,' they replied in unison.

'Exactly. And when you have gone out to eat or to watch movies, filled petrol in your vehicle, looked at buying clothes, appliances or other goods, or paid your child's school and tuition fees or bought medicines or paid hospital fees, what is the trend in their prices—increasing or decreasing?' he asked.

'Always increasing,' this time the entire audience replied in unison.

'Do you get it now? Our cost of living is steadily increasing. This constant increase in prices is called inflation. And like termites eat wood, its only purpose is to eat away the value of the money you earn and save.'

'So, although you are happy that you are putting in a lot of effort to save money and keep it in your savings account or in FDs and RDs to earn compound interest, the force of inflation works towards negating it.'

'But, how much is this inflation every year?'

'On average it is 4 to 5 per cent a year. Sometimes it's more and at other times it is less. And it may be less for groceries and more for education and healthcare. But overall, over a long period of time, prices have been increasing at 4 to 5 per cent a year on average. In simple terms, if you have a 100 rupee note today, it will only be worth 95 to 96 rupees in a year. So, in real terms, your money is losing value every year. In other words, your purchasing power is reducing.'

'But doesn't the interest that our bank pays on our savings account, FDs and RDs account help us to overcome inflation?'

'Let's see. Bank savings accounts are currently paying 3 to 4 per cent, which is less than inflation. And FDs and RDs are paying 5 to 6 per cent, which is slightly higher than inflation. But, you also need to take taxes into account as you have to pay tax on the interest you receive from the bank. This reduces your returns.

'So, if we assume a 33 per cent tax rate, then after tax, a savings account is only giving you a 2 to 3 per cent return and FDs and RDs are giving you a 3 to 4 per cent return. In effect, both are giving an after-tax return that is less than inflation.'

'Do you mean to say my money has been losing value all this time?' the middle-aged man who had been happy and proud about himself asked despondently.

'Unfortunately, that's true,' Siddharth told him.

Several audience members were also in the same camp and there were some murmurs in the audience.

'But, what's the solution?' one of the ladies asked.

'That's where we come to the fifth principle of financial planning which is that, after the basics are taken care of through your savings account, emergency fund, and FDs or RDs for your short-term goals, you have to invest in products where the expected after-tax return will be higher than inflation.'

The audience was silent for a while. Then someone asked, 'From where will we get such returns?'

'Will it be safe?' someone else added.

'We are middle-class people. We can't afford to take risks and lose money,' a third person clarified.

'That's where we enter the world of asset allocation, mutual funds, stocks, bonds, gold, real estate and other asset classes,' replied Siddharth with a smile. 'Various investment products are available that allow you to take risks commensurate with your risk appetite. But you need to be careful and not go overboard. Some people take too much risk, which is not suitable for them and end up losing money.'

'But we don't have sufficient knowledge of these investment avenues to take good decisions,' one of the audience members said.

'That's why it is advisable to work with a financial adviser. For a small fee, they can guide you so that the value of your savings is not only protected but can also grow to meet your goals whether it is a down payment for a house, buying a car, going on a vacation, your children's education and marriage, or your own retirement. If you want to meet these goals, you first have to cross the inflation hurdle,' Siddharth ended.

Takeaways

1. Inflation is the constant increase in prices. And just as termites eat wood, its only purpose is to eat away the value of the money we earn and save.
2. We should aim to invest in products where the expected after-tax return will be higher than inflation.

11

What is Your Core Competency? Mutual Funds

What is Your Core Competency?

'Our next speaker is Siddharth. He is a well-known financial adviser here in Mumbai and he will enlighten us about the basics of mutual funds.'

Siddharth was attending a gathering organized by a leading mutual fund house at a hotel in Mumbai. The speakers for the evening included a spiritual guru to energize the audience, followed by Siddharth to talk about the basics of mutual funds and finally a fund manager from the fund house to talk about the philosophy of the fund house, the process they followed and their fund performance.

The spiritual guru spoke about the need for meditation in the current stressful times and explained the difference between mindfulness, which is about being aware in the present moment, and heartfulness, which is about finding a source of love and calmness within your heart. He captured the attention of the audience with several examples and also managed to entertain them with some anecdotes.

After the emcee's introduction, Siddharth went on stage.

'Good evening, everybody. It's great to be here with you today. Swamiji just explained how meditation can help you relax and de-stress. I would like to take that one step further and talk about how you can become financially independent and further reduce your stress.'

Siddharth spoke briefly about the importance of being financially independent and how it was important that they enjoy this journey. He also talked about asset allocation and the basic principles of financial planning.

'We'll start by thinking about how we can simplify our finances thereby reducing a lot of stress in our lives. Let me start by asking you a simple question: What don't you want as investors?'

The audience seemed a bit confused. Whenever they had attended such sessions in the past, it was always about what investors wanted. This was the first time someone had asked them what they didn't want.

There were a few moments of silence. Then someone said, 'I don't want an empty bank account,' amidst laughter.

'Yes, you are on the right track. What does it mean for you as an investor?'

'I don't want to see any loss on my investment,' someone else answered.

'Excellent. That's the answer I was looking for,' Siddharth exclaimed. 'Let me tell you a short story.'

'Once, Rahul Dravid, the famous cricketer, was going in to bat and had a look of intense concentration on his face. A TV commentator asked him, "You are very focused; I am sure you must be thinking of whether you will score a century or a double century in this match, correct?"

'"Not at all," answered Dravid. "You are completely wrong. Actually, all I am thinking about is how I should not get out on the first ball. And once I achieve that, then all I think about is how I can score my first run, then five runs, then a double-digit score, and then twenty-five runs, fifty runs, and so on. If I can do that, then the centuries and double centuries will come."

'And that is the ideal approach for us too. As an investor, your top priority is to not get out on the first ball, which means that you should not lose money. Because once you get into a hole financially, it's very difficult to come out of it. And, after an unpleasant experience, you will not want to be an investor again. This is the concept of always putting risk before return. Understood?'

'Yes,' the audience answered in unison.

'Great. I am glad we got that out of the way right in the beginning. Now, let's come to the scoring runs part. What do you want as investors?'

'I want high returns,' said a young person.

'Okay. But what exactly does "high" mean?' Siddharth quizzed the audience.

'15 per cent, 20 per cent, 25 per cent,' he heard various answers. The young people in the audience especially seemed to have the highest expectations for returns.

'That's like saying you want to score a century or double century in every match. It may happen a few times but definitely not in every match. Similarly, you may see these high returns once every few years. But, do you really think you can get these kinds of returns consistently? How many of you have made such high returns on your investments consistently?' he asked.

There was silence in the audience.

'Let me tell you something. Only a handful of investors in the world have made these kinds of returns over the long term.'

'So, let me ask you again. What kind of return do you think you can *realistically* get over the medium to long term?'

'8 per cent, 10 per cent, 12 per cent'; again he heard multiple answers. This time, the middle-aged people in the audience made their voices heard. They were indeed more realistic than the youngsters.

'Actually, it's not an absolute answer. For most investors, getting a return that is 2 to 3 per cent per annum higher than the interest rate on an FD is a realistic target. If they can achieve that, they can easily beat inflation and protect the value of their savings, which should be their primary goal. And if they are patient, they may even see some better returns over the medium to long term, which will be sufficient to build wealth and meet their goals. And for most investors, a balanced asset allocation is the ideal solution to achieve this,' Siddharth said.

'But how do we get a balanced asset allocation?' an extremely enthusiastic lady in the first row asked Siddharth.

'That's what this session is about. And, I will try to make it as interactive as possible instead of a one-way monologue. So, please feel free to ask lots of questions as we go along,' Siddharth replied.

'Now, for a majority of the population, mutual funds would be the ideal investment product to achieve a balanced allocation with the least hassle,' he continued. 'They are ideal because they can give you diversification even if you have a limited sum of money to invest.'

'How do they do that?' the lady persisted.

'Mutual funds can do that because they combine the savings of a large number of investors, which is then managed as a single pool of money.'

'But who manages the money?' the audience wanted to know.

'Mutual funds are managed by professional fund managers who make the investment decisions so that individual investors do not need to worry about which stocks, bonds, commodities or other assets to buy. Mutual funds charge a small fee from investors for this service.'

'Can't we do this on our own?' a youngster who was taking notes asked Siddharth.

'You can try. For example, many people try to invest directly in stocks on their own but only a few are successful while the rest may end up with losses. However, the majority of the population does not have the time, interest or capability to research investment options, make a decision on the best choices to invest in, and time the entry and exit right. Mutual funds enable them to get the benefit of a diversified investment portfolio with minimum effort.'

'You mentioned that mutual funds would help to de-stress our lives. How do they do that?' asked a person sitting in a corner.

'Investing in mutual funds is advantageous as everyone can get on with their lives and focus on their line of work while ensuring that they protect the value of their savings and build wealth. For example, professionals in jobs, folks who have their own businesses, doctors, athletes, etc., can focus on their core competency while leaving the job of investing to the professionals. That way they have one less thing to worry about, and that implies lower stress, right?'

'But what if we don't have large sums to invest? There must be some minimum limit, right, because of which many of us won't be eligible?' a lady asked nervously.

'Not at all. In most funds, one can start investing with as little as a few hundred rupees a month.'

'Once we invest, will we be able to get our money back when we want it?' the questions continued.

'Of course, unlike many other investment options, mutual fund investments are highly liquid and can be redeemed whenever you need your funds. Most of the mutual funds don't have any lock-in period although they may charge a small exit fee if one redeems within a year of investing the money.'

'How difficult is it to start investing in them?'

'Mutual funds are very convenient to invest in. You can invest online with a direct debit from your bank account. Similarly, when you redeem, the funds are deposited directly into your account in up to three working days.'

'How can we invest in mutual funds? Can you explain the process in a little more detail?'

'You can invest directly through the asset management company or AMC, or through a distributor. You can go to the AMC's website and select the fund you want to invest in. The advantage of going directly is that it has a lower expense ratio or fee. The disadvantage is that you need to be knowledgeable about mutual funds, be able to evaluate their performance, select between thousands of funds and decide which ones to invest in or exit. Here, having a financial adviser will be beneficial as they can help you invest directly in a select set of funds that will be a good fit for the financial plan that they would have prepared for you. Here, you should note that a financial adviser has a fiduciary duty towards their client and is expected to take decisions in the best interest of their client.

'You can also go through distributors like banks, brokers, financial advisory companies or individuals who are registered as intermediaries with the Association of

Mutual Funds of India (AMFI). In this case, the expense ratio or fee will be slightly higher than if you go directly since the intermediary gets a commission but they can guide you on suitable funds to invest in. You should note that their advice is incidental and it is your responsibility to ensure that the funds you invest in align with your goals.'

'Do we have to make a one-time investment or can it be done on a periodic basis?'

'The process is very flexible. You can make a lump-sum investment at any time. However, for retail investors like yourself, it's recommended to follow a systematic investment plan or SIP. You can set up an SIP for a fixed sum of money like a few hundred or thousand rupees, or even a larger amount if you please, at a fixed frequency, for example, every month.'

'Why is an SIP better?'

'There are two benefits. One is that it introduces discipline to the investing process. Investors typically try to time the market, but most are very bad at it. They end up buying when the market rises and exit in a panic when the market falls. Hence, they end up buying high and selling low, which is the exact opposite of what they should be doing. An SIP automates the investment process and prevents investors from acting against their own interests.

'Secondly, with an SIP, investors end up investing a fixed amount every month irrespective of the level of the market. So, they do what is called rupee cost averaging. It means that if the market goes down, they end up with more units of the mutual funds they are buying. So, when the market goes up, they could get higher returns. Investing a lump sum amount also has a risk as investors could end up putting in the money when the market is at a high and any fall in the markets would lead to a loss.'

'Other than the expense ratio, are there any other charges we need to be aware of?'

'Most mutual funds have an exit load. Which means that if you sell your fund units within a specified time period of buying them, typically one year, you will be charged 1 per cent of the amount invested. This is meant to motivate investors to invest for the long term and not invest in mutual funds on an opportunistic basis, which can be detrimental to their investment returns.'

'What is the taxation for mutual funds?'

'Taxation is different for equity mutual funds, which invest in stocks and debt mutual funds, which invest in bonds. If you sell your equity mutual fund units within one year of purchasing them, you will incur a short-term capital gains tax of 15 per cent on any profits. And after one year, you incur a long-term capital gains tax of 10 per cent on any profits.

'For debt mutual funds, if you sell the units within three years of purchasing them, you will incur short-term capital gains tax as per your applicable income tax rate on any profits. And after three years, you incur a long-term capital gains tax of 20 per cent with indexation benefits on any profits. What it means is that your purchase price will be adjusted to reflect the effect of inflation for the time period you remain invested. Effectively, your adjusted purchase price comes out higher and the calculated profits are lower because of which you end up paying lower tax.'

'But, aren't there a large number of mutual funds? How are we supposed to choose between them?'

'That's an excellent question and it will take some time to cover the topic. But you can simplify your life by just taking the help of a financial adviser, who for a small fee, can choose the right funds for you.

'Else, you can go ahead and do this on your own too, if you think you have the interest, capability and time.

'But as I told you earlier, think about risk first and then about returns. Remember that mutual funds are subject to market risk,' Siddharth said as his session came to an end.

Mutual Fund Types: Debt, Hybrid, Equity and Gold

A few days later, Siddharth was invited to his building society's office on a Sunday morning.

'Okay. We have a quorum now. Let's begin the meeting,' Mr Shah announced as everyone shuffled into the society's office.

Mr Shah was the secretary of the housing society in which Siddharth lived, in Andheri. He was a retired businessman, having turned over his business to his children. He devoted his time to religious activities and took an active part in running the society. The managing committee, which consisted of five members, used to meet every Sunday morning. Although Siddharth had been living in the society for the past ten years, he had not played an active role in society matters or attended any meetings.

'Sure. But let me make myself comfortable first,' said Mr Patel as he put some jalebis and fafda—a Gujarati snack—on his plate. Mr Patel was an amiable, portly fellow with a sweet tooth who ran his own business. A few other committee members followed his example and helped themselves to the snacks.

Once everyone had settled down, Mr Shah continued, 'As you all know, at the last meeting, we had decided to explore some investment options for the excess funds which our society has collected from its members. Today, I have requested a special guest to join us. Siddharth and his family live in flat B-1203. He is a registered financial adviser and has a well-reputed practice here in Mumbai. I think he would be the best person to explain to us the various investment avenues we can consider. He has graciously agreed to spend time with us today.'

'Thank you, Siddharth.' All the committee members were very appreciative.

'It's my pleasure to be here today. As you all know, as individuals, we can invest in various asset classes such as savings accounts and FDs, stocks (domestic, international, emerging markets, etc.), bonds (corporate, government, high-yield, etc.), gold, real estate, currencies (or forex), commodities, etc.'

'Yes. We all have investments in some of these asset classes,' Mr Raman replied. He was the treasurer and knew all the numbers.

'Some of these like currencies and commodities are high-risk and are not suitable for our society. Others like FDs are low risk but will not help us beat inflation. And real estate is more of a long-term investment which is not a good fit for us,' Siddharth continued.

'That leaves us with stocks, bonds and gold, which make sense,' Mr Paranjape said. He was a practical, no-nonsense man who was responsible for the society's maintenance.

'But aren't these risky too?' asked Rupal Mehta, the fifth committee member. She organized all the cultural events for the society.

'Yes. That's why I would suggest that we go with mutual funds and not invest directly in stocks and bonds or buy physical gold. And it's important that we have a balanced asset allocation,' answered Siddharth.

He spent the next fifteen minutes explaining the basics of risk versus return, asset allocation and mutual funds. Some of the members were familiar with a few of these concepts and helped him in that regard.

'Siddharth, you have given us a good overview of mutual funds,' said Mr Shah, as he poured a cup of tea and handed it to Siddharth. 'From what I understand there are many different types of mutual funds. Can you please explain them to us?'

'Thank you,' said Siddharth as he had a sip of hot tea and felt energized. 'There are various types of mutual funds on the risk–return spectrum like debt, hybrid, equity, gold and passive. Let's look at them one by one.'

Debt Funds

'Debt funds or fixed income funds invest predominantly in rated debt or fixed income securities, that is, corporate bonds, debentures, government securities, commercial papers and other money market instruments. Debt mutual funds have the lowest risk and correspondingly offer lower but stable returns, which are slightly higher than bank FDs.'

'We have read in the news or heard of people who invested directly in corporate FDs and got burnt. How are debt funds different?' Mr Paranjape asked.

'Basically, those folks lent money directly to some companies and those companies defaulted on their payment obligations. To reduce this risk, debt mutual funds pool together investors' money and invest it in the bonds of hundreds of companies. Essentially, they are lending money to these companies. But even if any one particular company defaults, it doesn't impact their returns as much. So, it is better to invest in debt mutual funds as it provides diversification rather than investing in corporate FDs directly.'

'Okay. But aren't there many types of debt mutual funds?' Mr Raman pointed out.

'Yes. There are ten categories of debt funds based on the type of securities invested, residual maturity of the securities they invest in, and the credit risk of the securities. However, it is better for investors to stick to a few basic categories,' Siddharth responded.

'But how should we choose which categories to invest in?' Mr Raman persisted.

'You should do that based on your investment time horizon,' Siddharth started to explain.

'For short-term investments, that is, three to six months, you can invest in liquid funds or money market funds. Liquid funds and money market funds invest in highly liquid money market instruments and provide easy liquidity. Liquid funds are short-duration funds and are typically used by corporate houses, institutional investors and business houses for deploying surplus liquidity for a shorter period. Liquid funds are like your bank savings account. You can instantly redeem up to Rs 50,000 a day or up to 90 per cent of your money in the liquid fund, whichever is lower.

'For the medium term, that is, six to twelve months, you can invest in ultra-short-term funds. They typically carry lower levels of risk, but investors need to keep track of their holdings regularly to ensure that they have not invested in lower quality bonds to boost returns.

'For the longer term, that is, one to three years or slightly longer, you can invest in corporate bond funds, banking and public sector undertaking or PSU debt funds, short-term funds, or low-duration funds. Corporate bond funds are relatively safe as they predominantly invest in investment-grade bonds. Banking and PSU debt funds predominantly invest in bonds of banks, public sector undertakings, public financial institutions and municipal bonds. Short-term funds and low-duration funds may take some credit risk, so investors need to track their holdings regularly but their exposure to interest rate risk is lower.'

'Many fund houses offer debt mutual funds in these categories, right? How should we choose from among them?' Mrs Mehta inquired.

'It is usually safer to stick with the large funds from well-known fund houses,' Siddharth answered.

'What about the remaining categories of debt mutual funds?' Mr Patel asked Siddharth while biting into a jalebi.

'There are various other categories of funds like credit risk funds, medium-term plan funds, G-Sec funds, dynamic bond funds, etc. However, for our society funds as well as for investors who are starting on their investment journey and do not have sufficient knowledge of debt, it's best to stick to the basics. These other categories are best left to be considered by financial advisers or experienced investors who understand the risk,' Siddharth explained.

Hybrid Funds

'Next on the risk–return spectrum come the hybrid funds, which combine equity and debt. The value proposition is that the debt portion provides stability while the equity portion provides the upside, but also introduces some risk,' Siddharth started.

'Whom would hybrid funds be suitable for?' asked Mr Shah.

'They would be suitable for investors who typically have a more moderate risk profile. For example, this may be someone who has been investing mainly in debt but now wants to increase their risk exposure by introducing some equity in their portfolio. Also, if someone wants to invest in equity but prefers lower volatility in performance, they can choose hybrid funds as they are less volatile than pure equity funds.'

'How should we choose the right hybrid fund for us if we wanted to invest in them?' asked Mr Raman while taking some notes.

'There are six categories of hybrid funds based on the balance of debt and equity that they maintain. For example, there are aggressive funds that can invest 60 to 80 per cent in equity and the remaining in debt. They have the highest volatility. Then there are balanced funds which can invest 40 to 60 per cent in equity and the remaining in debt. As per their name, they try to give a more balanced exposure and have lower volatility than aggressive funds. There are also conservative funds that can invest 20 to 40 per cent in equity and the remaining in debt. These have lower volatility than balanced funds. Investors can choose the appropriate one based on their risk profile.'

'What is the advantage of these funds?' Mr Paranjape inquired. 'Can't we just invest in debt funds and equity funds separately?'

'The advantage is that these funds dynamically change the allocation between equity and debt based on market conditions,' Siddharth explained. 'So, if stocks have run up and valuations are high, they reduce the equity component and increase the debt component, and vice versa. That way, they not only reduce volatility but can potentially give a higher return and benefit investors.'

'Oh, I understand now,' said Mr Paranjape.

Equity Funds

'After that come the pure equity funds,' Siddharth came to his favourite part. 'Equity funds invest a major chunk of the corpus in equity securities with the main objective of providing capital appreciation over the medium- to long-term investment horizon. They are high-risk funds and the returns are linked to the performance of capital markets. Equity funds have the highest risk but can also provide the highest returns over the medium to long term.'

'Who are they suitable for?' Mrs Mehta wanted to know.

'Equity funds are for investors who have a moderate to high risk profile and who have an investment horizon of more than three years and ideally five to fifteen years.'

'Aren't there many categories of equity funds?' Mr Raman asked.

'Yes. There are fourteen categories of equity funds based mainly on the size (market capitalization) of the companies that these funds invest in.

'For example, some funds invest in large-sized companies, others in mid-sized or small-sized companies, while some invest in companies of all sizes. Some funds invest only in companies in a particular sector, such as technology, pharmaceuticals and healthcare, or banking and financial services, while other funds invest in companies that fit a specific theme, such as next-generation technologies or lifestyle and consumption, etc.'

'What is the advantage of investing in equity funds?' Mr Patel inquired.

'Over a medium to long timeframe, equity funds have historically given the highest returns among all asset classes. They typically give the best chance of beating inflation and growing your corpus.'

'I've also heard of equity-linked savings schemes or ELSS funds. What are they?' asked Mr Paranjape.

'Within equity, ELSS is a special type, which consists of all funds that are compliant with Section 80C of the Income Tax Act wherein you can get a tax deduction for your investment,' Siddharth explained patiently.

'That was a very good overview, Siddharth,' said Mr Raman, 'I thought I knew a fair bit about mutual funds, but you explained everything so nicely. I've learnt something new today.'

'Yes, you covered quite a bit today and you explained everything in such a simple way that I could follow,' Mrs Mehta was very appreciative.

'Can you give us a minute, Siddharth?' Mr Shah requested, 'There's something I want to quickly discuss with the other committee members.'

'Of course, sir. No problems at all,' said Siddharth. 'I'll just step outside for a minute.'

After a couple of minutes, Mr Raman requested Siddharth to join them again in the office.

'Siddharth, we appreciate the time you took today to explain various investment options in a simple language that all of us could understand,' said Mr Shah. 'It gave us a lot of confidence.'

'I am happy I could be of help,' replied Siddharth.

'We have one more request. If you would consider it, it would make our lives a lot easier,' Mr Shah continued.

'Please feel free to tell me, sir. I'd be happy to be of service,' Siddharth said.

'Would you consider being the society's financial adviser and managing our investments? We couldn't think of a better person for the job,' Mr Shah asked.

'Yes, Siddharth. I would really appreciate your assistance on this front. As you know, it's important that we manage the society's finances properly,' Mr Raman, the treasurer, said.

'Oh, I'd be happy to do that,' replied Siddharth. 'If I can play an active role in managing our society's investments, there'd be nothing like it. And I am happy to do it on a pro-bono basis.'

'Excellent, thanks, Siddharth. We appreciate it,' the committee members applauded him.

Takeaways

1. Investors should always put risk before return. For most investors, getting a return that is 2 to 3 per cent per annum higher than the interest rate on an FD is a realistic target. And for most investors, a balanced asset allocation is the ideal solution to achieve this.
2. For the majority of the population, mutual funds would be the ideal investment products to achieve

a balanced allocation with the least hassle. They can provide diversification even if investors have a limited sum of money to invest; as little as a few hundred rupees a month.

3. A systematic investment plan (SIP) in which investors put in a fixed amount every month into mutual funds brings discipline to the process and also provides rupee cost averaging.

4. There are various types of mutual funds on the risk–return spectrum like debt, hybrid, equity, gold and passive. Debt mutual funds have the lowest risk and correspondingly offer lower but stable returns that are slightly higher than bank FDs. Equity funds have the highest risk but can also provide the highest returns over the medium to long term.

12

Equity Mutual Funds: The Path to Wealth Creation

Equity Mutual Funds

'Okay, I've given you a broad overview of the various types of funds. Which funds would you like me to cover in more detail?' asked Siddharth.

'Equity mutual funds,' was the unanimous answer.

'Alrighty, then. Let's delve deeper into the world of equity mutual funds ...' Siddharth said with a smile.

He was at his monthly session with new investors at a hotel in Dadar, Mumbai. As usual, he had spoken about the concept of financial independence and covered the basic principles of financial planning, the importance of having a balanced asset allocation, and how mutual funds could help in this regard. After he had covered the various categories of mutual funds, the audience expressed an interest in knowing more about equity mutual funds, which typically most retail investors were interested in.

'Okay. Let's continue,' said Siddharth. 'We spoke about the fact that equity funds have the highest risk but can also provide the highest returns over the medium- to long-term horizon. Hence, they can be the ideal vehicle for wealth creation for patient long-term investors.

'There are multiple categories of equity mutual funds such as large-cap, mid-cap, small-cap, flexi-cap, sectoral and thematic, etc.

'First, let's look at large-cap funds.'

Large-Cap Funds

'Let's do an exercise right now,' Siddharth told the audience. 'Name some household products we all use every day.'

The audience was quick to rattle out some names in categories such as soaps and shampoos, apparel, footwear, biscuits, consumer appliances, automobiles, etc.

'Excellent. Do you know which companies manufacture these products?'

The audience members yelled out the names of some of the well-known companies that manufactured these products.

'Great. Now, which are some of the IT companies that have made a name for themselves on a global scale?'

Again, the attendees provided responses quickly.

'And what about banks and financial services companies whose services we all use?'

The audience was ready and provided the names of some large, well-known banks.

'I am impressed to see that you all are well aware of these names. As you know, these are some of the largest companies in India. They are highly reputed companies with the best corporate governance practices. They have an excellent track record of generating wealth for their investors over long periods. I am sure all of us have heard of folks who have made a fortune by investing in some of the IT companies in the 1990s or in some of the banks in the last decade.'

'Yes, my neighbour bought his flat with the profits he made from his stocks,' one of the attendees said.

'Great. Don't you wish you also had a small ownership in these blue-chip companies that have lower risk, but which give steady returns? Large-cap mutual funds serve this purpose. They are equity funds that invest a bigger proportion of their total assets in large companies which fall in the top 100 companies according to market capitalization (market value of the company's outstanding shares). Hence, large-cap funds are able to better withstand a slowdown in the markets, generate regular dividends and provide steady compounding of wealth. They carry a lower risk as compared to other types of funds and are known to generate steadier returns.

'In the long term (around five to seven years), large-cap funds tend to offer good capital appreciation, even though the returns may be lower compared to mid-cap or small-cap funds. Hence, they are a good option for investors with relatively lower risk appetite and a long-term investment horizon.

'Let's take a look at the historical returns for some of the largest large-cap funds over various periods of time,' said Siddharth as he showed them some data on the screen.

'As we can see, in the longest timeframe of fifteen years, large-cap funds have given very good CAGR returns of 15 to 18 per cent. In the 5 to 10-year timeframe too, the CAGR returns have been between 11 and 14 per cent, which is decent. Short-term returns in the past one to three years are in the range of 8 to 16 per cent CAGR and they have been volatile.'

'So, should we just pick the fund with the highest returns?'

'It's not as simple as that. We also need to consider the risk that the fund managers are taking to generate those returns.'

'How do we do that?'

'We look at some metrics such as the Sharpe ratio and Sortino ratio, which provide us with the risk-adjusted returns as well as an indication of the maximum loss in the mutual fund's value during market falls,' Siddharth said as he showed them some data on additional metrics.

'How do we interpret these metrics?'

'Basically, we need to look for the funds that are generating higher returns for the risk being taken. When things take a turn for the worse, funds that take higher risk can underperform. Essentially, we are looking for funds with the highest risk-adjusted return rather than just the highest return.'

'Understood. What else do we need to look at?'

'After that, it is important that you are comfortable with the fund manager's style of investing. Some fund managers focus on growth, which can entail higher risk but provide higher returns, while other fund managers focus more on stability, which can give lower returns at lower risk. So, you need to try and understand how the fund manager thinks.'

'Oh, that's good to know.'

'That's why you can't select a fund just by looking at its returns over the past one to two years. Because you wouldn't know how that fund manager has generated those returns, what kind of risks they have taken, and how their investment style may play out under future market conditions.'

'Yes, we understand that now.'

'Once we shortlist a few funds based on these metrics, then we should also look at the portfolio holdings if possible, to get a better understanding of how the fund is positioned for current and future market conditions.'

'Oh, but we don't think we are knowledgeable enough to do that,' some members of the audience said.

'Don't worry. That's where the services of a financial adviser come into the picture,' Siddharth answered. 'A good financial adviser should be able to do this next level of analysis and ensure that only the best-positioned funds are selected for your portfolio and not just the ones that have given good returns in the past one to two years.'

'Thanks for explaining it to us in a simple way that we could understand,' the audience members responded.

'Next, let's look at other categories of equity funds. Do you know how many publicly listed companies there are in India?' Siddharth asked.

'1000, 2000, 3000,' the audience threw out various numbers.

'Well, there are more than 5000 listed companies in India. And out of them only around 1000 are active.

'The Securities and Exchange Board of India or SEBI, the capital markets regulator, has classified these companies as large-cap, mid-cap and small-cap. Can anyone tell me how this classification is done?'

'On the basis of their market capitalization,' one person answered.

'Excellent. Market capitalization is just the share price of a company multiplied by the number of its shares outstanding. So, if the share price is Rs 100 and there are ten crore shares outstanding, then the market cap will be Rs 1000 crore.

'The top 100 companies by market cap are classified as large-caps. These are the largest, stable companies. Many of them are blue-chips or high-quality companies. Typically, their market cap is higher than Rs 30,000 crore.

'The next 150 companies (ranked 101 to 250) by market cap are classified as midcaps. Their market cap is typically between Rs 8000 crore and Rs 30,000 crore.

'The remaining companies (ranked 250+) are classified as small-caps. Their market cap is usually lower than Rs 8000 crore.

'Earlier, we have covered large-cap mutual funds that invest in stable large-cap companies. Now let's look at mid-cap, small-cap and flexi-cap mutual funds.

Mid-Cap and Small-Cap Funds

'Mid-cap funds invest a minimum of 65 per cent of their assets in stocks of mid-cap companies, that is, those that are ranked 101 to 250 in terms of market capitalization. These companies also have been around for some time and many of them have a good track record too. Some of them even have the potential to grow into large-cap companies after a few years. This makes mid-cap funds an interesting option for growth opportunities with manageable risk. Over a five-year horizon, they can provide higher returns than large-caps.'

'Are mid-cap funds suitable for everyone?'

'Good question. Not all mid-cap companies successfully transition to large-caps. Some of them fail or stagnate. However mid-cap funds diversify this risk as they invest in multiple companies in this segment. Overall, mid-cap funds are suitable for investors with moderate risk tolerance.

'Next, we come to small-cap funds, which invest a minimum of 65 per cent of their assets in the stocks of small-cap companies, which are ranked 251 or below in terms of market capitalization. These are the smaller companies or new entrants in the market. Many of them play in a particular niche. Small-cap companies have a high potential for growth and the best of them manage to grow into mid-caps and then to large-caps. They also carry a higher amount of risk. However, one should remember that all large-caps started out as small-caps and grew over time. Over a five to seven-year horizon, small-caps can outperform mid-caps and large-caps.'

'Small-caps also seem to be an interesting segment. Who are they suitable for?'

'Actually, this is the highest risk segment as small-cap companies have a higher chance of failing. Small-cap funds are usually suitable only for investors with a high risk tolerance.'

Flexi-Cap Funds

'Large-cap, mid-cap, and small-cap funds are restricted by their category definition. However, flexi-cap funds have no restrictions. They have complete flexibility to invest in large-cap, mid-cap or small-cap companies. Hence, they can take better advantage of market conditions and also take tactical or opportunistic calls.

'Some flexi-cap funds invest largely in large-cap companies and hence provide more stability. While others are more aggressive and invest largely in mid-cap and small-cap companies, for growth. So, investors should be careful about which flexi-cap fund they invest in and ensure that it is in line with their risk profile and goals.

'Also, as fund managers of flexi-cap funds take opportunistic calls to either focus more on large-caps or mid-caps and small-caps, it can lead to higher volatility in their performance as compared to large-cap funds.'

'Who are flexi-cap funds suitable for?'

'They are suitable for investors with a moderate risk profile with a medium-to-long-term horizon. In a flexi-cap fund, the fund manager has complete freedom to invest across sectors and across large-cap, mid-cap and small-cap companies, depending on where they expect maximum gains,' Siddharth explained. 'This versatility makes flexi-cap funds most suitable for equity fund investors, as the job of stock selection is left completely to the fund manager, which is the very idea of investing in a mutual fund.'

'So, what have been the returns of flexi-cap funds in the past?'

'In the long term, which is ten to fifteen years, flexi-cap funds have given a 13 to 18 per cent CAGR return. In the medium term, which is five to ten years, they have given 12 to 16 per cent CAGR returns. While in the short term, which is one to three years, returns have been in the range of 6 to 16 per cent CAGR.

'A variation of this is the large-and-mid-cap category of funds, which are mandated to invest a minimum percentage (45 per cent) each in large-cap stocks and mid-and-small-cap stocks. So, they have less flexibility than flexi-cap funds but typically are more aggressive due to higher allocation to mid-and-small-cap stocks.

'Another variation, which has been recently introduced, is the multi-cap category of funds which are mandated to invest a minimum of 25 per cent each in large-cap, mid-cap, and small-cap stocks. They have less flexibility than the large-and-mid-cap category but are typically more aggressive as they will have a minimum 50 per cent allocation to mid-and-small-cap stocks.

ELSS Funds

'I have also heard of ELSS funds. What are they?' one of the audience members asked.

'ELSS or equity-linked savings scheme funds are a special type of flexi-cap fund. Any investment in ELSS funds is eligible for a tax deduction as per Section 80(C) of the Income Tax Act. Because of that, they come with a three-year lock-in, that is, you can withdraw your money only after three years.'

'Isn't the lock-in a disadvantage for investors?'

'Actually, it's the opposite. The positive aspect is that it helps investors maintain their discipline and not sell their fund units and redeem in a panic during market downturns.'

Sectoral, Thematic and International Funds

'So far, we have covered large-cap, flexi-cap, large-and-mid-cap, multi-cap and ELSS funds, which are all diversified funds as they invest in companies across various sectors and themes. And we have also looked at mid-cap and small-cap funds, which have a higher risk than the diversified funds. Now let's talk about thematic and sectoral funds,' Siddharth continued.

Thematic and Sectoral Funds

'What are some of the interesting themes or structural trends that come to your mind?' he asked them.

'Technology and digital,' someone answered.

'Excellent. Funds that focus on this theme invest in companies in IT software and hardware, media, telecom, as well as new technologies like artificial intelligence and machine learning, etc. The best part is some of these funds can invest in international companies also. So, you will find companies like Apple, Amazon, Microsoft, Google, Facebook, Netflix, etc., also in their portfolio, which are not available to invest in the Indian stock markets. These funds typically focus on high-growth companies.'

'Consumption and lifestyle,' another person said.

'Yes, these funds invest in companies that provide products that we use in our everyday life such as consumer staples, consumer durables, retail, banking and other sectors. Some especially focus on companies that will benefit from products that youngsters use. Given the large middle class in India, consumption should see consistent growth going forward, which should benefit these funds.

'Next, let's look at some sectoral funds. What are some interesting sectors that come to your mind?'

'Pharma and healthcare,' a few people said at once.

'Correct, funds focused on this sector invest in pharmaceutical companies, hospitals and diagnostic chains, companies providing medical devices, etc. These funds fall in the defensive category, that is, they do well and provide stability to the portfolio when the economy may be going through a downturn and other categories of funds may not be doing well.'

'Banking and financial services,' someone added.

'Yes, funds focusing on this sector invest in private and public sector banks, non-banking financial companies, insurance companies, asset management companies, brokerages, etc. Credit, or loans, is the lifeblood of an economy and when an economy grows, banks and other financial services companies tend to do well. So, in India, these funds are expected to do well as the economy grows.

'Now that we have looked at some examples of thematic and sectoral funds, let me ask you, what do you think their advantages are?'

'The companies they invest in may grow faster and hence these funds can give higher returns than diversified funds,' one person answered.

'Excellent. Anything else?'

'In tough economic conditions, funds like pharma and healthcare may not fall as much as other funds and hence give higher returns.'

'Correct. Now let's look at the other side. What do you think some of their disadvantages are?'

'Since these funds are not diversified, any downturn in the theme or sector they invest in can lead to heavy losses.'

'Correct. These are considered tactical investments, which means that the timing of entry and exit becomes very important so that you are not saddled with losses. It's like putting your eggs in one basket. So, you need to watch that basket very carefully. In that sense, these funds have a higher risk than diversified funds. Don't go by past returns alone while evaluating a thematic or sectoral fund.'

'How much of thematic and sectoral funds should we have in our portfolio?'

'It is advisable to have a core-satellite structure in your portfolio. The core, which can constitute 60 to 70 per cent of the portfolio, should have diversified funds such as large-cap and flexi-cap funds. And the remaining 30 to 40 per cent satellite portfolio can have mid-cap and small-cap funds as well as thematic and sectoral funds.'

'Let's go ahead and look at another interesting category of funds—international funds.'

International Funds

'As investors, do you think you should invest only in Indian stocks or in global companies too?'

'Invest in Indian stocks first and then in international ones,' a youngster in the audience answered.

'Correct answer. Well done. But let me ask you, why should we invest in international stocks?'

'Because it is advisable to diversify geographically.'

'Right. Geographic diversification allows you to build a diversified portfolio that has the potential to capitalize on the strength of different countries. For example, the US is good in technology, China, Korea and Taiwan are good in manufacturing, and India is good in services.'

'Because it can help us to overcome currency depreciation.'

'Very good. Emerging market currencies generally have a long-term depreciation bias. For example, the Indian Rupee has been depreciating at 2 to 3 per cent every year against the US dollar. Investing globally enables currency diversification and benefits you when the rupee depreciates as you will get a better exchange rate when you redeem your units of international funds. Anything else?'

There was silence in the audience.

'It also enables economic diversification. One country can never top the charts consistently. At a macroeconomic level, most countries have their own economic cycle. For example, at some point, the US may do well; at another point, China may do well; and at a different point, India may do well. Hence, by investing in different countries, you can experience smaller crests and troughs in your returns.

'Another important aspect is that international investing gives you access to themes that are not available in India, whether it is advanced technologies such as AI and machine learning, automation and robotics, cloud computing, nanotechnology, biotech, genomics, etc. You can invest in leading-edge companies in the world, which is not possible in India at this time.'

'This sounds interesting. How can we invest internationally?

'You can invest in international funds. They are usually diversified across countries, sectors and themes.'

'What are the risks?'

'Remember that there are risks to international investing too. For example, a particular country may go through a downturn or the rupee can appreciate in value unexpectedly, etc.'

'How much of one's portfolio should be in international funds?'

'You can invest up to 10 per cent of your portfolio in international funds.

'So, I hope you all have got a good overview of various categories of equity mutual funds by now. Happy investing,' Siddharth said as his session came to an end.

Takeaways

1. There are multiple categories of equity mutual funds such as large-cap, mid-cap, small-cap, flexi-cap, large-and-mid-cap, multi-cap, sectoral and thematic, international, etc.

2. Large-cap equity funds invest mainly in large companies that fall in the top 100 according to market capitalization. They are a good option for investors with a relatively lower risk appetite and a long-term investment horizon.

3. Mid-cap and small-cap funds invest a minimum of 65 per cent of their assets in stocks of mid-cap and small-cap companies, respectively. They provide exposure to growth opportunities with manageable

risk and are suitable for investors with a moderate to high-risk tolerance.

4. Flexi-cap, large-and-mid-cap and multi-cap funds are diversified funds that have the flexibility to invest in large-cap, mid-cap and small-cap companies. Hence, they can take better advantage of market conditions and also take tactical or opportunistic calls. They are suitable for investors with a moderate risk profile with a medium-to-long-term horizon.

5. Sectoral and thematic funds as well as international funds can be considered for tactical allocation. They can provide higher returns but also come with higher risk.

6. It is advisable to have a core-satellite structure in our portfolio. The core, which can constitute 60–70 per cent of the portfolio should have large-cap and diversified funds. And the remaining 30–40 per cent satellite portfolio can have mid- and small-cap as well as thematic and sectoral, and international funds.

13

Simplify Your Life: Index Funds, ETFs, Fund-of-Funds

That weekend, Siddharth got together with his Indian Institute of Technology (IIT) classmates in Mumbai. They used to meet once every few months. Most of the time, they would just get together over dinner and drinks. But sometimes, there would be a specific topic that the group would be interested in and they would have a special Sunday session. One of them would present on the topic, following which there would be a lively, freewheeling discussion.

This time, the topic of interest was investments. And Siddharth had been nominated to lead the discussion. As usual, he had spoken about the concept of financial independence and covered the basic principles of financial planning, the importance of having a balanced asset allocation and how mutual funds could help in this regard. After he had covered the various categories of mutual funds, his classmates expressed interest in knowing more.

'I have been hearing a lot lately about index funds and ETFs. What are they?' Shrikant asked.

'These are called passive products,' Siddharth responded. 'Let me explain.'

Passive Funds—Index Funds and ETFs

'Warren Buffett, the famous investor, has said: "A low-cost index fund is the most sensible equity investment for the great majority of investors. By periodically investing in an index fund, the know-nothing investor can actually outperform most investment professionals,"' said Siddharth.

'Is that true for investors globally?' an inquisitive Shrikant asked.

'Now that's especially true in developed markets like the US where the equity markets have matured, and fund managers find it difficult to perform better than the overall market. But, it may not hold in emerging markets like India where the equity markets are still inefficient and fund managers still have a chance to beat the market performance. This is especially true in the case of mid-and-small-cap stocks although in the case of large-cap stocks, it is becoming increasingly challenging for fund managers to beat their benchmark index,' Siddharth provided his rationale.

'But what exactly are index funds?' Shrikant wanted to know.

'Index funds invest only in companies that are present in an index like the Nifty 50, Sensex, Nifty Next 50, etc. These fall in the category of passive funds, which means that the fund manager does not actively decide which stocks to invest in but just invests in all the stocks in a particular index,' Siddharth said. 'Essentially, index funds are just a basket of stocks that represent a broad market. In the case of a Nifty 50 index fund, you're buying a small piece of the fifty largest publicly traded companies in India,' Siddharth explained.

'What is the advantage of buying an index fund?' Anand asked.

'It results in automatic diversification, which minimizes your overall risk,' Siddharth responded. 'Importantly, there's no market timing or individual stock picking involved—the fund simply tracks the performance of the stock index. So, it is ideal for investors to invest small amounts slowly over a long period of time. This is known as rupee-cost averaging and it's a sound strategy for most long-term investors.'

'I've heard that they have lower fees than other mutual funds. Is that correct?' Deepali, who had been silent for some time, put forth her question.

'Yes, you are right. Investors save on the fee they pay the fund house to manage their investments, which is typically a percentage of the total funds being managed. For example, if you invest in an index fund with a 0.25 per cent expense ratio, the fee will be Rs 2.5 for every

Rs 1000 of your total assets annually. This is typically lower than what other mutual funds charge, which can be 0.6 to 0.8 per cent for direct investment and 1.5 to 2 per cent for regular investment through an intermediary.'

'How is it possible for index funds to charge lower fees?'

'They are designed to be passive, that is, they just replicate the index, so they don't require much attention from fund managers. Hence, they can charge lower fees and make investing financially accessible to the masses.'

'However, as I mentioned earlier, investing only in index funds may not be the best idea in India. Do you know why?' asked Siddharth.

'Because we still have good investment opportunities in companies that are not in the index,' James volunteered.

'Excellent. That's one of the key reasons. India has a long runway for growth. So, fund managers can invest in companies that have good growth prospects but are not in the index yet. There's a good chance that such companies will perform well and may get included in the index one day. So, returns can be higher.

'Another reason is that Indian markets are still inefficient. What that means is that the valuations of companies may not always reflect their intrinsic value. So, it's possible that the companies in the index may be overvalued at some point in time while the rest of the companies may be undervalued. Hence, it may be better to invest in the non-index companies rather than in the index as returns can be higher.'

'We've also heard of ETFs. What are they?'

'ETFs are exchange-traded funds. Basically, they track an index, a commodity or a basket of assets as closely as possible, but trade like shares on the stock exchanges. They invest in stocks of companies, precious metals, etc., and are backed by physical holdings of the commodity.

'Their advantage is that they can be traded at any time like stocks and their expenses are much lower than the corresponding index funds. So, you can invest in the Nifty 50 ETF instead of the Nifty 50 index fund. Or you can invest in a technology ETF instead of investing in a technology fund.

'Overall, the key advantages of ETFs are trading flexibility, portfolio diversification, risk management and lower costs. Investors have the flexibility to invest in broad-based index ETFs as well as sectoral and thematic ETFs. So, it enables them to build a diversified portfolio as per their risk profile and at a low cost. That's one of the reasons ETFs have scaled up in developed markets like the US where ETF assets under management (AUM) is growing at a faster rate than mutual fund AUM.'

'Are there any disadvantages of ETFs?'

'First of all, to invest in ETFs you need to have a dematerialized (demat) and trading account with a stockbroker, either online or offline. Whereas for investing in mutual funds, you don't need a demat account.'

'Secondly, ETFs are still at a nascent stage in India currently and may not be very liquid. So, you may end up paying more in terms of transaction costs due to higher bid-ask spreads, which means that there is a large difference between the price the seller is asking for and what the buyer is willing to pay. Also, an ETF can have a tracking error versus the underlying benchmark index, which means that the returns from the ETF may vary from the returns of the underlying index it is supposed to track. These factors add up and can result in the returns being lower than if the investor had just invested in the corresponding index fund where the cost would end up being relatively lower.'

'There are ETFs that invest in physical gold and track the price of gold in real-time, right?' asked Deepali. 'I've always bought physical gold only. What is the advantage of buying a gold ETF versus physical gold?'

'There are a lot of advantages as you can buy and sell the ETF at any time at the current market price, you don't have to worry about purity or making charges, and you don't have to worry about storing your gold,' Siddharth answered as they wound up their discussion.

Fund of Funds—Keep It Simple

The next week, Siddharth addressed a virtual meeting over Zoom with individual retail investors. Many of them had logged in from smaller cities and towns in Maharashtra. He used to have such sessions every month and loved them as they gave him a chance to speak in a mix of Marathi and English.

'Good afternoon, everybody. It's great to have you all here for this session on Fund-of-Funds. I'll try and make this an interactive session,' he started.

'In my previous sessions, I have talked about the importance of asset allocation and how having a balanced allocation across stocks, bonds, gold and real estate is important to get stable returns that are higher than what you would get if you put all your savings in FDs.

'We've also looked at how mutual funds are a good way for you to invest in different asset classes. However, some of you have called me or sent me messages that investing in mutual funds is still a bit challenging for you. So, let me ask you—what are some of the issues you face?'

Many of the attendees voiced their issues.

'Not all of us have access to good financial advisers. There are thousands of funds across multiple categories and we don't know how to choose from them.'

'We need to monitor and keep track of the performance of selected schemes.'

'From time to time, we need to decide whether to retain these funds or change funds in our portfolio.'

'We don't understand the tax implications of making any changes.'

'We get multiple statements from multiple fund houses and have to reconcile holdings across funds.'

Siddharth listened patiently to all of them.

'After considering the issues you are facing, I think you can evaluate a Fund-of-Funds or FOF. It provides a streamlined solution to the twin pain points of asset allocation and fund selection, and will simplify things for you.'

'But, what exactly is a Fund-of-Funds?'

'FOF is essentially a mutual fund that primarily invests in other mutual fund schemes and ETFs. Its primary objective is to generate returns through diversified investment styles of the underlying schemes, while at the same time reducing overall volatility.'

'How is it better than if we directly invest in mutual funds ourselves?'

'There are multiple advantages to a Fund-of-Funds as follows.

'One, affordability. It allows investors even with limited capital to tap into a diversified portfolio of schemes with different underlying assets. Investors can even start an SIP in FOFs with a few hundred rupees and their money will be invested in all the underlying mutual funds held in the FOF portfolio.

'Two, professional management. A dedicated portfolio manager is responsible for the initial asset allocation, constant monitoring and regular rebalancing. And they try and select the best mutual funds based on historical risk-adjusted performance, the fund manager's track record, how the funds are positioned for expected market conditions, etc. The portfolio manager may have a better chance of selecting funds that may outperform than individual investors can. So, investment in FOFs can provide better risk-adjusted returns and at the same time, make an investor's life easier.

'Three, significant cost saving. Typically, when investors sell their funds to rebalance their portfolio, they have to pay tax on any gains. However, in the case of a Fund-of-Funds, there is no tax impact of rebalancing of the underlying schemes in the FOF portfolio as mutual fund schemes are exempted from capital gains tax. Also, the FOF invests in direct schemes of mutual funds and in ETFs. So that reduces overall costs. Do note that as per SEBI regulations, all FOFs are taxed as debt funds, that is, at the slab rate for short-term capital gains (if sold before three years) and at 20 per cent with indexation for long-term capital gains (if sold after three years). However, as the long-term capital gains tax on equities is also 10 per cent currently, the tax on long-term capital gains on FOFs is not significantly different from equities.

'Four, lower volatility. Due to the negative correlation between various asset classes like equity, debt and gold, and diversification even within one asset class, FOFs typically have lower volatility.

'Lastly, convenience. Investors have less documentation to go through. And the time needed for review and bank account reconciliation is also significantly reduced.'

'Great. That seems to solve most of our problems.'

'Yes, FOFs can help to simplify your life and investments.

'In addition, FOFs provide flexibility which is a key differentiator. For example, some FOFs can invest in four different asset classes—domestic equity, international equity, debt and gold. Domestic and international equity provide exposure to growth while debt and gold provide stability and liquidity.'

'Who are they suitable for?'

'They are suitable for everyone. Some of the FOFs come in three flavours—aggressive, moderate and conservative, targeted to investors with different risk profiles. Each of them has a different allocation to various asset classes.

'First is the aggressive FOF. It has a higher allocation to equity mutual funds and ETFs, a smaller allocation to debt and some allocation to gold.

'Second is the moderate FOF. There is moderate allocation to equity mutual funds and ETFs as well as moderate allocation to debt and some allocation to gold.

'Third is the conservative FOF. There is lower allocation to equity mutual funds and ETFs, higher allocation to debt and some allocation to gold.

'In addition, there are also some FOFs that invest in international mutual funds and ETFs. So, they can give investors international exposure too.'

'How can we be sure that the portfolio manager is following the right process to select the mutual funds in the portfolio?'

'Good question. Typically, the portfolio manager follows a comprehensive process covering both quantitative and qualitative factors. They have a model that helps in decision-making for both asset allocation as well as fund selection. They aim to select the best mutual funds based on historical performance, the fund manager's track record, how the funds are positioned for various market conditions, etc.'

'This was very helpful. We were not aware that this solution to our problems was available,' said many of the attendees.

'I thought so. That's why I highlighted this today. I'd recommend that you evaluate FOFs in more detail as it will make investing easy for you,' Siddharth said as the session came to an end.

Takeaways

1. Index funds invest only in companies that are present in an index like the Nifty 50, Sensex, Nifty Next 50, Bank Index, etc. These fall in the category of passive funds, which means that the fund manager does not actively decide which stocks to invest in but just invests in all the stocks in a particular index.

2. ETFs are exchange-traded funds. Basically, they track an index, a commodity or a basket of assets as closely as possible, but trade like shares on the stock exchanges. They invest in stocks of companies, precious metals, etc., and are backed by physical holdings of the commodity.

3. A Fund-of-Funds (FOF) is essentially a mutual fund that primarily invests in other mutual fund schemes and ETFs. Its primary objective is to generate returns through diversified investment styles of the underlying schemes, while at the same time reducing overall volatility. It provides a streamlined solution to the twin pain points of asset allocation and fund selection.

14

The Stock Market Beckons: Ben Graham's Principles

The Stock Market Virus—Is There an Antidote?

Siddharth finished his morning walk on a Sunday and headed to a nearby Starbucks where he was supposed to meet his friend Amar for coffee.

Amar, who worked at a stock brokerage firm was already there, reading the morning newspaper.

'Get this,' he said excitedly, pointing to a chart in the newspaper. 'The CSI 300 Index on the Shanghai Stock Exchange has risen 14 per cent in five days, with a return of 5.7 per cent in a single day. The daily turnover now exceeds \$213 billion for the first time since 2015.'

'Really? That's interesting. But, can we at least order a coffee and something to eat first? I am hungry,' said Siddharth.

'It seems Chinese social media has exploded with searches for the term "open a stock account",' Amar continued, ignoring Siddharth's appeal.

'Really? What is so different in China?'

'Well, the advance is also being aided by an enthusiastic chorus from the nation's state media. A front-page editorial in *China Securities Journal* recently said that fostering a "healthy" bull market after the pandemic is now more important to the economy than ever.'

'Oh. So, the government is encouraging this. After all, you have to give people something to keep them distracted from the pandemic, I guess,' Siddharth reasoned. 'And what's a better adrenaline boost than the stock market?'

'No need to be sarcastic, Siddharth. People need something to do when they are sitting at home. And anyway they are not able to spend money on other activities. So, why not on the stock market? This is good for the brokerage business,' Amar said, as he finally got up from his seat and went to the counter. 'What do you want to order?'

Siddharth got himself a cappuccino and a butter croissant while Amar ordered an iced latte and a scone for himself. As they settled into their chairs and took a sip of their coffees, the discussion went back to the increased retail participation in the stock markets.

'It seems that a similar frenzy for stock market investment among retail investors has been witnessed in Thailand too,' Amar added. 'Some 1,46,250 people opened new trading accounts for the first time this year through May, according to data from the Stock Exchange of Thailand. That exceeded the total number of new stock investors for all of 2019.'

'This seems like the stock market virus is spreading now after the coronavirus,' Siddharth laughed.

'You are right,' Amar couldn't control his laughter too. 'The virus seems to have reached the US too. Brokerages Charles Schwab, Interactive Brokers and TD Ameritrade added more than 1 million new accounts in the first quarter, a 4 per cent increase from the previous period. A year ago, that increase was about 1 per cent.'

'The US stock markets are up too, right?'

'Yes. The headline indices like the Dow Jones and S&P 500 had fallen almost 40 per cent from their highs but have rallied over the past month. They are close to their pre-Covid levels while the tech-heavy Nasdaq index is at an all-time high.' Amar brought up a stock chart on his phone. 'Although some studies suggest that the impact on US stock market performance on account of the retail investor participation may not be that significant.'

'And what about India? Our stock indices have rallied over the past month too, right?'

'Yes. The Nifty had fallen almost 35 per cent from its February high. But it has rallied too and is now at an all-time high.'

'Has retail participation increased in India too?'

'Yes. We are seeing the same trend here. Brokerages have seen an increase in the number of people opening trading accounts. And institutional participation in the market has reduced while retail participation has increased.'

'So, it's the same phenomenon here? People sitting at home with nowhere to go and nothing to do getting some action in the stock market?'

'I guess that's the case. We also saw that the non-Nifty stocks have done well over the past month. And mid-caps and small-caps have done better than large-caps. All these are signs of increased retail participation in markets.'

'But, do retail investors understand what they are getting into?'

'I can't vouch for that. We do provide them with a lot of educational material but it's every man and woman for themselves.'

'Investors need to understand that stock trading is like a high-risk adventure activity they are doing without wearing a safety harness or having a safety net below. So, they should only risk the money that they can afford to lose.'

'But, what is the antidote to this stock market virus? Do you think retail investors can follow some rules in this regard?'

'There are only two basic rules which Warren Buffett has put very aptly.

Rule No. 1: Don't lose money.

Rule No. 2: Don't forget rule no. 1.'

'You are right. I hope retail investors remember that and don't get into trouble,' Amar said. 'I believe it is critical to educate people about the pitfalls of direct investment in the stock market and after that, if they still want to go ahead, then they need to be educated about how they should go about evaluating stocks.'

'Absolutely. But I also think awareness about various investment solutions and products is higher than before,' Siddharth replied. 'And with investor-friendly regulations, the introduction of transparent and investor-friendly products, ease of investing, digitalization and a perception of mutual funds as long-term wealth creators, more and more investors may gravitate towards mutual funds.'

'Yes, you are right to some extent, but there's still a long way to go,' Amar responded as they got up and left for their homes.

As Siddharth reached his home, he vowed to educate as many people as he could so that they could invest wisely and not fall by the wayside on their journey to financial independence. He thought about the best way to do it and decided that he needed to educate investors about some of the basic frameworks for evaluating stocks. He knew he couldn't do it alone. But, he knew where he could enlist some help.

The Intelligent Investor

'Okay, now that we are all here, we can start,' Vedika announced, calling the meeting to start. Everyone settled down in chairs that were laid out in a circle. They had gathered at a small room of a local club where she had a membership.

'Good evening and welcome to the first meeting of the Investors Book Club,' she continued. 'As you all know, we have formed this club to motivate ourselves to read, review and discuss the concepts of the best books on finance and investments.'

There were five participants at the first meeting—Vedika, Siddharth, Alice, Mandar and Prabhat.

'We will aim to meet at least once every month, correct?' inquired Mandar.

'Yes. Every member will recommend a book and take the lead to organize the meeting to review that book,' Vedika replied, 'Today, we will review the book *The Intelligent Investor* by Benjamin Graham, which I had recommended. Did everyone like it? Warren Buffett has recommended it as the best book that investors can read.'

'You gave us quite an assignment. It's a 600-page tome,' Prabhat joked and everyone laughed.

'Yes, but I also gave you a hint of where to focus,' Siddharth pitched in with a smile. 'Warren Buffett has highlighted that it has only three ideas that we really need:

1. **A stock is a piece of a business**—Keep in mind that we are buying a business that has an underlying value based on how much cash goes in and out.
2. **Mr Market** (Chapter 8)—The market quotes us prices that we can take or leave. Nobody is forcing us

to accept Mr Market's offer. So, we should make the stock market serve us and not the other way around.

3. **Margin of Safety** (Chapter 20)—Always buy a business for way less than we think it is conservatively worth.'

'Yes. I must admit that your hint helped us focus our time and effort. Thanks for that,' Vedika replied.

'Great. Let's start then, shall we?' Siddharth said with some excitement.

A Stock is a Piece of a Business

'I'll begin,' said Alice. 'Graham has pointed out that as retail shareholders, we have a dual status. On one hand, we are a minority shareholder or a silent partner in a business. We rely on the promoter or the management team to run the business. Our returns are entirely dependent on the profitability of the company or on a positive change in the value of its underlying assets.

'On the other hand, as we typically only hold a very small stake in the business, we can sell our shares at any time we wish in the stock market. The price, though, fluctuates constantly and often may be nowhere close to the value of the underlying business. Unfortunately, given that we all now have access to stock-market apps at our fingertips, we now rely more on stock price movements to determine how well a business is doing and rarely consider ourselves as a partner in the business.'

Partnering with Mr Market

'That's right, Alice,' Mandar continued. 'On our investment journey, our partner is Mr Market and he is not stable but manic-depressive! He has a split personality. He can be euphoric one moment and miserable the next. And since we have easy access to the stock market now through our smartphones, he is our constant companion and insists on telling us every day what our interest in a business is worth, depending on his mood.

'In addition, he doesn't sit still. He offers to either buy our stake or to sell us an additional interest in the business every day, which is really not needed and leads to a problem. Sometimes, his assessment of a business's value appears somewhat accurate and justified by how the business is doing, recent developments in the economy and the future outlook. However, given his split personality, often Mr Market lets his enthusiasm, or his fears, run away with him and the price he quotes for a business seems far removed from reality.'

'But the key to being a successful investor is to understand that as investors, we need to have an independent mind, think for ourselves and not get swept by Mr Market's mood,' said Prabhat. 'We shouldn't become euphoric or miserable just because he thinks so. We should control our emotions of greed and fear. Unfortunately, most investors fall into his trap and fail in their investment journey.'

'Absolutely right,' said Siddharth. 'As investors, our biggest strength should be our independent thinking.

Instead, if we permit ourselves to be governed by what Mr Market thinks our stocks are worth and act according to what he tells us, we are transforming our basic advantage into a disadvantage.'

'An analogy that is easy to understand is that we don't call a real estate agent every minute to check the market price of our flat or house,' Vedika continued. 'And even if they provide a quote, we wouldn't rush to sell what we own or buy another one. By not checking, or even knowing, the market price of our flat or house from minute to minute, we are in no way preventing its value from changing over time.'

'The takeaway is that Mr Market's job is to provide us with prices and distract us, but our job is to remain focused on business value and decide whether it is to our advantage to act on the price quotes,' said Alice. 'We do not have to trade with Mr Market just because he constantly begs us to. We can succeed in the long term only by controlling our emotions, refusing to buy assets at inflated prices or sell at rock-bottom prices, diversifying across asset classes, and controlling our transaction costs and taxes.'

'Excellent, I think we have covered the parable of Mr Market in detail. Let's look at margin of safety next,' Vedika said.

'Well, we need a short snack break before that, don't we?' Siddharth asked, with a glint in his eye.

'Oh, you got something for us?' everyone asked.

'Of course,' said Siddharth as he opened his backpack and took out some packets of jalebi and fafda. Everyone pounced on them.

'Hey, didn't we just talk about controlling our behaviour?' Vedika exclaimed as everyone enjoyed themselves.

Margin of Safety

After their brief snack break, everyone assembled back to continue their discussion on Ben Graham's book *The Intelligent Investor.*

Vedika started them off. 'In a legend, a monarch once asked the wise men in his court to invent for him a sentence, to be ever in view, which should be true and appropriate at all times and situations. They presented to him the words: "This too shall pass."

'In the same way, Benjamin Graham has distilled the secret of sound investment into three words: "Margin of Safety".

'Essentially, it is ensuring that the intrinsic value of any asset we purchase such as a stock, bond, etc., is always higher than the price we pay for it. The margin of safety is what we can count on to protect us from loss in the event of an unexpected future decline in the business.'

'That's an excellent summary, Vedika,' Prabhat said. 'The key thing is to understand how the margin of safety is calculated. In the case of bonds, we should look at the *past* ability to earn profits in excess of interest expense and not rosy future projections. For example, if the pre-tax profit is a multiple of the interest expense that a company would need to pay on its loans, then there is a margin of safety.

'Alternatively, we can compare the total enterprise value with the total amount of debt. For example, if a business owes Rs 100 crore but is worth Rs 300 crore, there is room for shrinkage of two-thirds in business value before the bondholders suffer a loss. This amount of extra cushion is the margin of safety.'

'And in the case of stocks, one of the ways to evaluate the margin of safety is to look at the expected earnings yield, that is, the inverse of the Price-to-Earnings (P/E) ratio, and see if it is considerably above the bond yield of the company,' Siddharth continued. 'For example, if the P/E ratio of the company is 11x, then its earnings yield is 9 per cent. If the company's bonds, or other similar company's bonds, are yielding 7 per cent, then we have a 2 per cent margin of safety, which can prevent or minimize a loss in case the earnings decline.

'On the other hand, if the company's bonds are yielding 10 per cent and the earnings yield is only 9 per cent, then we don't have any margin of safety and we are basing our investment on an assumption that the profits of the company will increase significantly in the future, which may or may not happen.'

'In addition, diversification is an established tenet of conservative investing and complements the margin of safety principle,' Vedika continued. 'So, if we build a portfolio with a diversified list of twenty or more stocks, each with a margin of safety, then the loss on any one of them is still manageable and the probability that our overall portfolio will be profitable becomes quite high.

'The risk, though, is that many investors have concentrated portfolios of a few stocks. And worse, they purchase stocks when the going is good and the stock market is at relatively high levels. Or, in their enthusiasm, they buy low-quality stocks where the chance of earnings decline is high. Some even buy unprofitable stocks just based on a rosy narrative.'

'You are right,' Alice said. 'I know many investors who purchased low-quality stocks or initial public offerings, IPOs, at times when business conditions were good temporarily. They assumed that the current strong earnings trajectory translates to sustainable earning power. However, such stocks do not offer an adequate margin of safety as their profits can decline dramatically when business conditions change. Many investors have been burnt by investing in high-flying stocks that turned out to be junk.'

'There is a risk in high-quality stocks too, though. In this case, investors end up paying too high a price for good-quality companies by just going with an optimistic narrative. For example, in current times, investors are focused on buying growth stocks whether it's in technology, healthcare, consumption or banking and finance, and they find it difficult to apply the margin of safety principle,' Vedika continued.

'As a buyer of growth stocks, we rely on expected earnings growth that is *higher* than the average in the past. And typically, we get swept away in the market's enthusiasm and extrapolate recent growth. It just becomes a lazy exercise in an Excel sheet. However, we have to be careful to project future earnings conservatively and ensure that the calculated intrinsic value shows a satisfactory margin of safety in relation to our purchase price. We have to remember that the margin of safety is always dependent on the price paid. It will be large at one price, small at some higher price, and non-existent at some still higher price.

'The margin of safety principle is a cornerstone that distinguishes an investment from a speculation,' added Prabhat. 'Anyone who buys a stock on a view that the market is going up or down cannot be said to be protected by a margin of safety. It's just speculation. To qualify as an investment, a true margin of safety based on the stock price versus the intrinsic value of the business must be present.'

Investment vs Speculation

The discussion on the margin of safety had been quite interesting and exhausting and the book club members—Vedika, Siddharth, Alice, Mandar and Prabhat—had taken a short break. After some time, Vedika brought the discussion back to *The Intelligent Investor*.

'We've covered the two most important chapters in the book—Chapter 8 on Mr Market and Chapter 20 on Margin of Safety. But there is a lot more to learn from Graham, isn't there?'

'Absolutely. The first and most important choice any person can make in the stock market is whether to be an investor or speculator,' Prabhat said. 'If we want to speculate, we should do so with full knowledge that the probability that we will lose money will be high. In that case, the best approach is to keep our funds for speculation separate from our funds for investment, so that we can limit any losses.'

'But how do we know whether we are an investor or a speculator?' Siddharth asked.

'If our emphasis is on *timing*, which means we are trying to anticipate or forecast how the stock market will move, that is, to buy and hold when we think stocks will go up or to sell and refrain from buying when we think stocks will go down, we are a speculator,' Prabhat clarified.

'So, what differentiates an investor?' Siddharth continued his line of questioning.

'As an investor, we should focus on the business and not on the stock markets. Our analysis should be based not on the stock price but on data and facts, which can lead to the valuation of a stock. We should then compare our estimate of the value with the current market price to determine whether or not we should act to buy or sell a stock,' Prabhat responded.

'The key for any investor then is to focus on value rather than price,' Siddharth summed up. 'No wonder Buffett has said, "Price is what you pay. Value is what you get."'

'That also highlights the importance of diversification,' added Prabhat. 'As investors, it is natural for us to go with our gut feel and bet big on a stock that we *know* is going to be highly profitable, rather than diversify across multiple stocks, which can dilute our returns. But we cannot just take a concentrated bet on a few stocks, because accurate valuation of a business cannot be done *dependably and our gut feeling can be wrong*. It happens all the time. Hence, it is critical to build a diversified portfolio of stocks.'

'If we follow these guidelines on the margin of safety and diversification, and avoid speculating, are we assured of a good performance in the stock market then?' asked Alice.

'There are no guarantees in the stock market. Any stock can go up or down by 40 to 50 per cent in a short span regardless of whether the market as a whole goes up or down. This could happen due to a change in macroeconomic conditions or business fundamentals. Stock markets can be very volatile, and we need to have the stomach to tolerate the ups and downs to be a successful investor,' Mandar answered. 'The most successful investors don't just have a strong mind; they have a strong stomach.'

'There are other behavioural aspects that we need to keep in mind,' Siddharth added. 'As investors, we always plan to buy low and sell high, but nobody can time the market perfectly. The stock market's behaviour is a random walk. It does not obey any rules.'

'So, what is the solution for average investors then?' Vedika asked.

'A better approach is asset allocation, that is, have a portfolio composed of asset classes like stocks, bonds, gold, etc., and change their proportion in the portfolio based on the level of the stock market,' Siddharth continued. 'This is called rebalancing. When the stock market goes up, we should reduce the level of equity in the portfolio and allocate more to other asset classes such as debt and gold and vice-versa.'

'Wow, asset allocation and rebalancing are what is recommended for most investors now. And Graham was suggesting that in the 1970s,' Vedika responded.

'It's pretty clear that Ben Graham was way ahead of his time!' everyone concluded.

'We've all spent some time to understand Ben Graham's principles and should apply it in our investing process,' Siddharth observed. 'But that's not enough. Each of us should pass on this knowledge to as many people as possible and ask them to pass it on as well. It's only through such a viral effect that people will invest in a disciplined and knowledgeable manner.'

'Very valid point, Siddharth,' everyone agreed as they got up to leave after a productive discussion. 'We'll do it.'

Takeaways

1. Investors need to understand that stock trading is like a high-risk adventure activity they are doing without wearing a safety harness or having a safety net below. So, they should only risk the money which they can afford to lose.

2. A stock is a piece of a business. We should never forget that we are buying a business that has an

underlying value based on its cash flow, i.e., how much cash goes in and out of that business.

3. We should make sure that we are buying a business for way less than we think it is conservatively worth, giving us a margin of safety.

4. The market quotes us prices that we can take or leave. Nobody is forcing us to accept Mr Market's offer. So, we should make the stock market serve us and not the other way around.

15

Multibagger Stocks: The Peter Lynch Principles

The Quest for Multibaggers

'Welcome, please come in,' Sharad Joglekar, the editor of a local newspaper in Pune, invited Siddharth into a room.

'Thanks,' said Siddharth as he entered a waiting room next to a large auditorium at Kothrud, Pune, where the newspaper had organized a seminar on investments for their readers on a Sunday.

'You know we have a fairly large readership here. And we frequently get questions from the public on various topics. So, we organize seminars on the most popular ones. One of the most common topics our readers want to know about is investments and stocks. Since you frequently talk on these topics at your seminars, we thought it would be good to invite you. Our readers would love to hear from you,' said Sharad.

'Yes, of course. It's my pleasure,' replied Siddharth. 'There's nothing like stocks to capture people's attention.'

A waiter brought in some tea and a plateful of hot batata wadas. 'Please have some. It's a Pune speciality as you know,' Sharad said with a smile.

'Oh, I can't resist these, 'Siddharth said, as he had a couple of wadas with tea. They were delicious.

After a few minutes, an assistant came in. 'Sir, the auditorium is full now. We can start,' he informed Sharad.

'Okay. Shall we start then?' Sharad asked Siddharth, who replied in the affirmative.

As they entered the auditorium, Sharad was surprised to see more than 500 people in the audience. There were men and women, people across all age groups from young to middle-aged folks as well as older people who would have been retired. Some had also brought their teenage children to the session.

When Siddharth glanced at the screen, he understood why. There, in big bold letters, was written the topic for the day: 'Identifying Multibaggers in the Stock Market.'

Not many people would be able to resist coming to such as session, even if it's on a Sunday evening, Siddharth thought to himself with a chuckle.

After a brief introduction, Siddharth rose to speak. As he liked to keep his sessions interactive, he started with a question.

'How many of you have heard about Warren Buffett?' he asked.

Almost 80 per cent of the audience raised their hands.

'How many know the name of his company?'

Around 50 per cent of the hands went up. Some folks answered, 'Berkshire Hathaway.'

'Okay. How many people here can name three companies in his portfolio?'

Only around ten hands were raised this time. They were able to provide satisfactory answers.

'That's good. I will ask one final question. Buffett has one chocolate manufacturing company in his portfolio. Does anyone know the name of the company?'

This time only one person raised his hand. 'See's Candies,' he answered with confidence.

Siddharth was pleased. 'Excellent. You are a true Buffett fan. I have a special prize for you. Please collect it from me at the end of this session,' he said amidst applause from the audience.

'Now I started this talk by referring to Warren Buffett because he is one of the most successful investors in the stock market. And there is a lot to learn from him.'

'But do you know the basic rules he has emphasized for investors?' he asked as he showed a slide on the screen.

Rule No. 1: Don't lose money.

Rule No. 2: Don't forget Rule No. 1.

'All of us should keep this in mind during our journey in the stock market. What this means is that the stock market is not a one-way ticket to making a fortune. Success is not guaranteed. Many times, stocks can fall by 40 to 50 per cent in a short period of time. Hence, you should invest directly in stocks only if you can overcome your fear in such situations and not sell in a panic. In fact, in some cases, investors can lose all their money too. Remembering this can help us avoid taking unnecessary risks in the hopes of making quick money. Does everyone understand this?' he asked and got an affirmative response from the audience. He could see the disappointment on some of the faces.

'Also, bear in mind that you cannot invest in stocks just based on stock tips, or what you read in the newspaper, or watch on business news channels. You will need to think on your own and do your own due diligence on companies. The good part is that now a lot of information and resources are available for free on the Internet to enable you to do this if you indeed want to. But you should think of investing directly in stocks only if you have the capability, time and inclination to do so. Else it would be best if you invest in index funds and mutual funds, and leave the stock-picking to the professional fund managers. Is that understood?' he asked.

'Yes,' the audience answered, but he could see the disappointment on more faces and some murmurs in the crowd.

'Okay. So, let's first understand what equity means and what a stock is. Can anyone tell me, please?'

'A stock is a share in a business. So, when you buy a stock, you are part owner of the business,' a member of the audience replied.

'Correct. And why does it make sense for us to own stocks?'

'Because we can own a small piece of outstanding businesses which we would have no hope of owning otherwise. And we can do that even if we have small amounts to invest and can build up our stake over time.'

'Excellent. What else?'

'We can own stocks in fifteen to twenty different businesses across sectors. So, we can get the upside but also reduce our risk because of diversification.'

'Very nice. Go on.'

'We always have the flexibility to vote with our feet and exit a stock if we are not happy for any reason.'

'Awesome. All are very valid points. We should always bear in mind that a stock is not just a piece of paper or a symbol flashing on your computer screen. Actually, it represents your share, however minuscule, of a real business. If you keep this in mind, it will help you to think long-term.'

'But some people claim to make short-term profits too with stocks, correct?' someone asked a question.

'Yes, but they are traders. And trading may not be suitable for most individual investors or amateurs. Unless a trader is really very good, they end up losing money most of the time,' Siddharth replied.

'Just to be clear, what we will be discussing here is identifying stocks which can be multibaggers, that is, rise five, ten, twenty times or more but over the long term. Is that understood?' he continued.

'Yes,' the audience replied in unison.

'Great. Let's continue then. If a stock represents our share in a business, and we want to invest in stocks that will be multibaggers over the long term, then what kind of stocks should we invest in?

People in the audience shouted out the names of some well-known companies.

'Excellent. These are all what we would call high-quality companies and they all have been multibaggers over the past ten to twenty years. Most of them started as small companies and grew to become some of the largest companies in the country today. But is our quest just to invest in these well-known names?' he asked.

There were some confused faces in the audience.

'No, it's not. Some of these companies may well continue to be multibaggers but others may not. So, we need to keep an open mind and find companies that can be multibaggers over the next decade. Some of them can be small companies today, but what we need to see is if they have the potential to grow their business and profits over the next decade or more,' he continued.

He saw quite a few heads nodding in agreement.

'But how can we find such companies? Isn't that the job of professional fund managers?' one of the audience members asked.

'For that, we need to keep in mind the guidance that Peter Lynch, one of the greatest investors of all time, has given in this regard,' Siddharth replied. 'Let's see what he said.'

The Peter Lynch Principles

'Even as an individual investor, you can look at identifying stocks for investment on your own,' Siddharth continued. 'But bear in mind that you should have the interest, capability and time to do the research and monitor your investments, as well as have the courage to take tough decisions in difficult circumstances. Else, it's best to leave this to the professionals.'

'So, should we continue or stop here?' he teased the audience.

'Continue, continue,' the audience replied as one.

'Okay. In that case, Peter Lynch, one of the most successful mutual fund managers in the world, has provided some excellent guidance which we can all heed.

'You can find terrific investment opportunities in your home, neighbourhood or workplace, months or even years before professionals identify them. Your edge is in taking advantage of what you know.

'Let's do an exercise right now. What are some brands of products or services you use, which are popular in general and which you believe are high quality or you can't do without?'

'Colgate toothpaste, Dove soap, Pantene shampoo, Parachute, Harpic, Lizol, Rin, Ariel, Godrej products, Fevicol, Asian Paints,' the audience yelled back a number of names.

'What about in the food segment?'

'Pizza Hut, Domino's Pizza, McDonald's, Daawat rice, Fortune oil, Nestlé Maggi, Red Label tea, Nescafé, Amul milk.'

'In clothing and footwear?'

'Pantaloons, Zara, H&M, Nike, Adidas.'

'In discretionary items like smartphones, cars, ACs, etc.?'

'Apple iPhone, Samsung phone, Bajaj, Hero, Maruti, Hyundai, Honda, Mercedes Benz, BMW, LG, Blue Star, Havells.'

'What about the youngsters in the audience? What are some names that come to your mind?'

'WhatsApp, Instagram, Twitter, LinkedIn, Facebook, Zoom, Microsoft, Amazon, Google, Netflix, Disney,' the youngsters in the audience mentioned their favourites.

'Excellent, many of the companies that sell these products have been multibaggers. Similarly, there will be other products which are also good, but the companies that provide them are not so well-known yet. For example, I have identified a small packaged foods company whose products my daughter likes, and I have seen many youngsters buying at the stores in our neighbourhood.

'Let me give you another example. Nine years ago, I was flipping channels on TV when Salman Khan came on for an ad for Hawaii chappals. I was intrigued as to why a company selling chappals had Salman Khan in their ad and how they could even afford him in the first place. So, I read up about the company and was amazed at its financial performance and the track record of its management. I also bought their brand of chappals, tried them out and found them to be good quality. So, I went ahead and bought their stock. Not only am I holding on to those shares till now, but I have added to my position over time. And believe me, it's turned out to be a multibagger!

'So, at your home and workplace, keep track of the products and services that you, your family members or colleagues use that stand out in terms of their quality or functionality. And when you go out anywhere next time, keep your eyes and ears open for products, retail stores or restaurants that you or your family members like or which seem exceptionally popular. That can be your first step to identifying potential multibaggers.'

'Is it really that easy?' a young person in the audience wondered.

'This is just the starting point. Bear in mind that liking a product, store or restaurant is only a good reason to get interested in a company and put it on your research list as a lead. However, it's not enough reason to own the stock. Never invest in a company before you've done the homework on a company's business, financials, growth prospects and risks. Is that clear?'

'Yes. What would the next step be?' an audience member asked eagerly.

'You will need to do a bit of reading and have some knowledge of financial analysis for the next step. First, you will need to go through the past three to five years of annual reports, any recent quarterly reports and conference call transcripts, and presentations of the company to make sure you understand the business model, strategy, management track record and financial performance. The idea is to see if you can spot something special about the company or what is called sustainable competitive advantage.'

Siddharth heard a groan from the audience. Some heads drooped. He could see that some of the audience seemed lost.

'All the information is freely available on the Internet. But how many of you think you would be able to do this basic analysis?' he asked. Less than half of the audience raised their hands.

'Well, you'll need to learn some basic financial analysis if you want to pick stocks on your own. Else, it would be better for you to just invest in mutual funds or find a financial adviser who can help you in that regard. Investing in stocks directly is not for everyone, just as everyone can't be a doctor, pilot, architect or an engineer.'

'In the next step, you need to evaluate key financial metrics such as 1) Sales growth, 2) Profit margins, 3) Earnings growth, 4) Dividends, 5) Cash flow, 6) Return on equity, 7) Return on invested capital, 8) Cash position, 9) Debt, 10) Inventory, 11) Hidden assets/liabilities, 12) Pension plans, 13) Book Value, 14) P/E multiple, 15) Stock buybacks, etc.

'That's too much for someone who doesn't have any background in finance,' someone yelled out.

'We have full-time jobs too. How can we spend so much time on this?' another person asked.

'As I said earlier, you need to have the interest, capability and time to do this kind of analysis. Else it would be best if you just invest in mutual funds or get help from a financial adviser. It's just like when you fly in an airplane, you don't fly the plane yourself, do you, even if it feels exciting? You leave it to the pilot.'

'In that case, isn't it easier to just listen to the experts on the business news channels or read the business newspapers?' a third person asked.

'If you do that, you will likely be the last person to know about the investment idea. Remember that if you are looking for multibaggers, you need to invest in companies before they come on the radar of other investors or even the professionals. Once everyone jumps in after hearing about it on the business news channels or reading about it in the newspaper, the stock becomes a multibagger.'

He could see that a majority of the audience was realizing that this was not their cup of tea. But others seemed interested and wanted to know more.

'Okay. Let me simplify things a bit more then. If all this seems too much and you can follow only one bit of data, follow a company's earnings, that is, their profits. Sooner or later, earnings make or break any investment in the stock market.

'How many of you feel that you are capable of doing this analysis on your own?'

Less than 10 per cent of the audience raised their hands this time.

'Okay, Let's go on. What we'll discuss now should still help everyone here . . .' Siddharth continued.

The Peter Lynch Framework

'According to Peter Lynch, companies can be categorized as:

1. **Slow growers:** Large and ageing companies whose earnings (i.e., profits) are growing in line with the growth rate of the economy, which may be 5–7 per cent. Due to limited growth opportunities, they often pay regular dividends. These fall in the low risk–low return bucket.

2. **Medium-growth stalwarts:** Large companies that are clocking annual earnings growth rates of 10–12 per cent. They fall in the low-risk–moderate-return bucket.

3. **Fast growers:** Small, aggressive new companies with annual earnings growth rates of 20–25 per cent. These fall in the high-risk–high-return bucket.

4. **Cyclicals:** Companies whose sales, profits and stock prices tend to move up and down in a predictable way along with the economic cycle or commodity cycle. These can be in the high-risk–low-return or low-risk–high-return bucket.

5. **Asset plays:** Companies with hidden assets, e.g., land, intellectual property, etc., where the value of the assets exceeds the company's market capitalization.

6. **Turnarounds:** Companies whose business has been beaten down but have the potential to recover. These fall in the high-risk–high-return bucket.

'Should we invest in multiple companies in these categories?' the audience asked Siddharth.

'You can aim to build a balanced portfolio with 30–40 per cent allocated to growth, 10–20 per cent to cyclicals, 10–20 per cent to asset plays, and the remaining to turnarounds. Keep in mind that this depends on economic and market conditions too.'

'But in which category will we find the multibaggers?' an inquisitive person asked.

'Fast growers—small, aggressive new enterprises that grow at 20–25 per cent a year—are the land of multibaggers. But the risk is also higher as their value falls rapidly if they falter. Look for ones that have good balance sheets, are making substantial profits and cash flow, are able to reinvest the cash to generate high returns and where management has a proven track record. The key is to figure out when they will stop growing and how much to pay for the growth.'

'Many times, I have seen that while we are searching for the next big thing, a company selling boring products or solving a basic problem grows big right under our nose without us realizing it,' another person said.

'A very valid point. Who would have thought that a company selling glue with a brand name would become a multibagger? So, don't go by first impressions. A fast grower's name can sound dull, or its business can seem dull, disagreeable or depressing. It can be a spin-off from a larger company, there may be rumours about it due to which its stock price may have fallen, or it can be in a no-growth industry. It may be a user of technology rather than a technology company itself.

A good sign of a multibagger is if the company has a niche in which it dominates and customers have to keep buying its products even if it increases prices. The institutional investors may not own it and analysts may not follow it because the company is small. And if the company is buying back its shares and if the promoters and management team are also buying its shares, it provides additional confidence.'

'Many times, we read or hear about some hot stocks that are supposed to become multibaggers. What is your view on those?'

'It's best to avoid the hottest stocks in the hottest industries, the 'next' somethings, companies diversifying into unrelated businesses and stock tips. Most of the time, these are sure-shot ways to lose your money.

'Do your research and develop your own narrative or story for the company and keep revisiting it every few months. Even if you can't predict earnings, you can find out how a company plans to increase its earnings. Then you can check periodically to see if the plans are working out.'

'Okay. Once we reach this point, then can we buy the stock?' asked an enthusiastic participant.

'Not yet. There is one final thing to factor in. And that is valuation. In terms of valuation, we can look at some key metrics like the Price-to-Earnings (P/E) multiple, Price-to-Book (P/B) multiple, etc. The key is to ensure that we have a margin of safety. For example, a simple thumb rule to follow is that the P/E multiple should be equal to, or close to, the long-term earnings growth rate. Avoid stocks where the P/E multiple is more than 2x of the earnings growth rate. And if the P/E multiple is half of the earnings growth rate, the stock may be a bargain.

'On the valuation front, you can make it as complicated as you want. But it would be best if you try and keep it simple at this time. Do keep in mind that good businesses may not always be available at reasonable valuations, that is, where the P/E multiple is close to its long-term earnings growth rate, especially in India where businesses get a premium for growth. So that's where subjectivity and patience come into the picture.'

'It seems easier to just watch the so-called experts on business news channels or read the stock tips in the newspapers,' one of the audience members said, leading to laughter in the audience.

'That will not help much. If you just sit around, follow and endlessly debate stocks, you are wasting your time. Predicting the economy or stock market is futile. Instead, focus on understanding company fundamentals and developing your independent view on whether the business is improving or deteriorating. This does entail putting in some time and effort but in the end, it will be worth it. Else you are just speculating.

'Hopefully by now, it's clear that investing directly in stocks may not be everyone's cup of tea. Remember that risk is not so much in the stock market or in the company as it is in the investor's behaviour,' Siddharth ended.

Takeaways

1. We should think of investing directly in stocks only if we have the capability, time and inclination to do so. Else, it would be best if we invest in index funds and mutual funds, and leave the stock picking to the professional fund managers.

2. We can start by evaluating companies that we know something about and whose products or services we use in our daily life. But we should never invest in a company before we've done the homework on a company's business, financials, growth prospects and risks. However, we need to invest in companies before they come on the radar of other investors or even professionals.

3. In the Peter Lynch framework, companies can be categorized as slow growers, medium-growth stalwarts, fast growers, cyclicals, asset plays and turnarounds.

4. Fast growers—small, aggressive new enterprises that are growing their profits at 20–25 per cent a year— are the land of multibaggers. But the risk is also higher as their value falls rapidly if they falter.

5. Risk is not so much in the stock market or in the company as it is in the investor's behaviour.

CHAPTER 16

Other Traditional Asset Classes: Gold, Real Estate

Gold as an Asset Class

The next week, on a Sunday, Siddharth was relaxing at home with his family.

'These bhajias are yummy.' He heartily helped himself to a second serving. Knowing fully well that he loved to eat fresh batata wadas and bhajias when the rains started, his wife, Shraddha, had made one of his favourites, onion bhajias, that day.

Siddharth took his plate of bhajias with tomato sauce and mint chutney and sat on his favourite armchair in the balcony. The monsoon had started, and it was raining very heavily that evening. He sat there staring at the raindrops that seemed to be falling almost horizontally now and listened to the howling wind and intermittent thunder. It was a perfect setting for having a piping hot fried snack.

'Did you see this? Gold has risen to almost Rs 50,000 per *tola* (10 grams) now,' his mother looked up from the newspaper and called out to him from the couch in the living room.

'Yes, ma. I've been tracking that,' Siddharth replied from the balcony.

'Hasn't it risen more than 50 per cent in the past year?' Shraddha yelled out from the kitchen. It was amazing how women always had a ear for gold. She came out from the kitchen with another plate full of fresh bhajias and called everyone to the dining table.

'If only your son had listened to me and bought some gold instead of investing it in his stocks and mutual funds,' Shraddha told Siddharth's mom.

'Don't worry,' Siddharth replied. 'I always maintain a balanced asset allocation and invest part of the savings in gold. In fact, that's what I tell my clients too.'

'But do you think it can go much higher from here?'

'Let's see,' Siddharth said as he brought up a chart on his iPad. 'Here's a chart of gold showing the long-term price trend over the past twenty years in USD/oz.

'Gold is now trading just above $1850/oz and has declined a bit after hitting a fresh eight-year high of close to $2300/oz a couple of months ago.'

'But what does the price of gold depend on?' Shraddha inquired, 'Why had it risen so much over the past year and do you think it will go higher?'

'That's a tough question to answer. It's not possible to assign any intrinsic value to gold. So, the price of gold is subjective,' Siddharth replied. 'Gold prices depend on the economic growth prospects, any risks such as the Covid-19 crisis, geopolitical developments such as the Russia–Ukraine conflict and global recession, as well as interest rate changes, currency movements, and speculation by traders.'

'Can you explain it in simple terms so all of us will understand?' Siddharth's mom asked him.

'Sure, ma. Every day when you are watching the news, you are seeing a lot of negative news about high inflation, global recession and the Russia–Ukraine conflict, correct?'

'Yes, it is making me depressed,' his mom replied.

'Exactly, this continued uncertainty is leading to negative sentiment in the market. And whenever that happens, investors rush to a safe haven asset whose value will not get impacted even during such crises. And gold is that safe haven asset.'

'Okay. But what about interest rates?' Siddharth's father, who was silently enjoying the bhajias all the while, finally spoke up. 'How do they impact gold prices?'

'The best factor that can explain the move in gold is real US bond yields or the interest rates. As yields fall, gold becomes more attractive as investors would rather put their money in gold to safeguard the value of their savings versus depositing it in the bank at low interest rates. During the Covid crisis, as concerns about the economy intensified, real rates headed lower, helping gold prices head higher. Now, as central banks globally are raising interest rates, gold prices are trending lower.'

'And currency impact?' his father continued.

'A weaker dollar drives up gold prices as it becomes cheaper for international investors to buy gold. However, the dollar has been strengthening for the past few months, which is negative for gold.'

'I've also heard of gold ETFs. What are they?'

'Gold ETFs make it easy for investors to invest in gold without any of the hassles of owning physical gold like purity concerns, storage cost, security, etc. Basically, investors buy gold ETFs and the ETF provider buys and stores the physical gold. Gold ETF inflows also remain a strong driver of gold prices.'

'Are there any other factors that impact gold prices?' his mother asked him.

'Yes, it is also important to look at demand from global central banks and from consumers in countries like India and China.

'To summarize, increased risk and uncertainty, opportunity cost and momentum drive gold prices.'

'As an investor, how much should one invest in gold?' Shraddha inquired.

'One can have anywhere from 5 to 15 per cent allocation to gold in their portfolio,' Siddharth replied. 'That can provide good returns if gold prices rise higher and also help to reduce the volatility of the overall portfolio.'

'And what's the best way to invest in gold?' Shraddha continued.

'The best way is to invest in gold ETFs. They are easy to invest in and also are liquid so that you can exit at any time you want.'

'Where can we buy these gold ETFs?'

'You can buy them in your demat account. The top mutual fund houses offer gold ETFs. So, you can invest in one of them. Also, the Government of India has launched a sovereign gold bond scheme that investors can consider. Remember that gold is a good hedge against inflation and also helps to reduce the overall volatility of your portfolio.'

'That's nice, Siddharth,' Shraddha said. 'You've explained this in a simple way that we all could understand.'

With that, their discussion came to an end. Everyone got an understanding of investing in gold as an asset class and had enjoyed the bhajias too.

Real Estate

The next week, Siddharth went to meet some of his friends in the financial advisory and wealth management business after his office hours. They met for dinner at Pa Pa Ya restaurant in South Mumbai, well-known for its Asian cuisine.

After general chit-chat and exchanging views on the stock market, they ordered some dim sums and sushi rolls for appetizers.

The discussion then turned towards real estate.

'From a diversification point of view, as an asset class, investors should think of having real estate in their overall portfolio. And we are not talking of the primary home here but buying property as an investment,' Manas started. 'However, the issue is that, as an investment option, real estate may have been attractive a decade ago when property saw good price appreciation. But if we see the returns over the past five years, they are not that encouraging. In fact, real estate has given a return CAGR of less than 1 per cent over the past five years and 3.5 per cent CAGR over the past ten years.'

'You are right. Real estate prices have been stagnant for the past five years. I invested in a flat in Kandivali a few years ago. Prices have gone up since then but when I calculated my return, it's much less than what I could have made by investing just in an index fund,' Amar lamented. 'Some of my clients are also in the same boat.'

'But the housing sector seems to be seeing a rebound,' Siddharth responded. 'The data shows that sales in Mumbai and Pune have risen ever since the government announced some measures specifically for the sector. Is it a good time for investors to look at the real estate sector as an investment avenue again?'

'But that is just in these two cities, right?' asked Shivani. 'What about other big markets like NCR, Bengaluru, etc.? And what about the rest of the country? I believe there is some improvement, but I don't think we are out of the woods yet.'

'Well, let's look at various factors that impact real estate prices,' Siddharth said. 'People seem to be feeling a bit more confident about their jobs and income with the economy on an uptrend. Prices have not moved much in the past few years. And with the Reserve Bank of India (RBI) reducing interest rates over the past two years, home loan rates are also lower than in the past. With the RBI starting to raise rates, home loan rates will also rise a bit. But overall, affordability levels have reached levels last seen in the 2000–05 period due to record low home loan rates and prices remaining stagnant for long.'

'Also, the real estate market is improving with government support in some states. Debt yields had fallen too although they have started rising now. So, with that investment option still not being very attractive, investor demand for property should increase,' Amar pointed out.

'Okay. So, I guess we can expect increasing interest in the real estate sector going forward. But with the inventory of saleable houses being so high, it may take some time for prices to increase significantly and for investors to get meaningful returns,' Manas said.

'That's true. But let's also look at other factors. The rental yield is just 2 to 3 per cent, less than what investors would make on an FD,' Shikha added. 'Not to mention the high maintenance costs and potential issues with tenants. In some cases, there are even documentation and legal issues. Is it even worth it?'

'And we must keep in mind that it should be considered as a high-ticket size but illiquid asset, that means investors can't exit it any time they like as they may not find a buyer at their price point,' Manas pointed out. 'It's not like a mutual fund or stock which we can sell any time if we need the money or just want to book profits.'

'We have all made some very valid points. I guess the demand for property is expected to rise but it's debatable if returns from real estate will match returns from other asset classes. But investors can consider it more as portfolio diversification. We've all seen time periods when stock markets have crashed but real estate has done comparatively well,' Manas summarized the discussion just in time for them to order their main course.

As everyone was in the mood to experiment, they ordered Japanese stir-fried noodles, Indonesian fried rice, Malaysian curry, Thai green curry and Chinese tofu. The food lived up to their expectations and their taste buds had a party.

'By the way, what do you guys think about Bitcoin? It had hit an all-time high of more than $69,000 per bitcoin but has fallen by more than 70 per cent to $20,000. Are you guys following it?' asked Shivani as they had their dessert.

Takeaways

1. Gold provides a hedge against inflation, recession and geopolitical tensions as well as volatility in markets and is an important component of asset allocation. Gold prices have a high negative correlation to US real bond yields.

2. Gold ETFs provide a convenient way to invest in gold. They are easy to invest in and also are liquid so that we can exit at any time we want.

3. Investors can consider real estate for portfolio diversification purposes. However, it is a long-term, illiquid asset, i.e., investors cannot exit it any time they like.

17

Fatal Attraction: Bitcoin

The discussion between Siddharth and his friends took an interesting turn over dessert.

Bitcoin—What Is It Exactly?

'Bitcoin is one of the most well-known cryptocurrencies, although there are others too, like Ethereum. Many speculators have been trapped in the ongoing correction,' Shiv, who had been listening silently all this while, responded with some excitement. He had an interest in technology and Bitcoin was up his alley.

'Oh, is that so? What exactly is the difference between a normal currency and a cryptocurrency?' asked Amar.

'Currency is typically issued by central banks. For example, the rupee is the currency issued by the RBI and the dollar is the currency issued by the US Fed. In contrast to that, cryptocurrency is a digital currency in which transactions are verified and records maintained by a distributed computer network rather than by a centralized authority. The network uses cryptography techniques that allow only the sender and intended recipient of a message to view the contents of the transaction,' said Shiv.

'But can we use it like any other currency?' Manas asked.

'Absolutely. Just like any currency, bitcoins can be exchanged for other currencies, products and services,' Shiv continued.

'If I have bitcoins, how would I actually spend them?' Shivani asked.

'Bitcoins can be sent from user to user on the peer-to-peer Bitcoin network without the need for intermediaries. Basically, I would just transfer my bitcoins from my online wallet to your online wallet,' Shiv explained. 'Transactions are verified by network nodes through cryptography and recorded in a public distributed computer ledger called a blockchain.'

'So, has Bitcoin gained broad acceptance as a currency?'

'Actually, central banks and regulators have stepped in to prevent widespread use and misuse of Bitcoin as a currency. Today, investors are looking at Bitcoin more as digital gold, that is, a store of value than as a currency. But we should note that Bitcoin prices themselves are quite volatile. And it has also not proven to be much of a hedge against rising inflation or geopolitical tensions in the past few months.'

'Tell me one thing. Are bitcoins safe? Or can a hacker steal them?' Amar wanted to know.

'Bitcoins use a combination of a public address and a private key,' Siddharth jumped in. He had done some research on this topic. 'For example, I can tell others a Bitcoin address or even make it public without compromising its corresponding private key, which only I will know. To be able to spend the bitcoins from my wallet, I would need to know the corresponding private key and digitally sign the transaction. The network verifies the signature using the public key. My private key is never revealed to anyone and computing the private key of a particular Bitcoin address is practically infeasible for hackers. So, the mechanism is safe.'

'Is it foolproof though?' Amar continued.

'Well, one has to be careful to remember one's private key. There have been cases where users have forgotten their private keys and lost access to their stored bitcoins. Or they stored their private keys on a USB drive and then misplaced it, thereby losing access to their bitcoins. And one has to be careful to keep the private key secret. If the private key is revealed to anyone, for example, through any data leaks or breach, then they can use it to steal the stored bitcoins,' Siddharth responded.

'Bitcoins have also come into controversy, right?' Manas asked.

'Yes, Bitcoins have been characterized as a speculative bubble. They have also been used as an investment, although several regulatory agencies have issued investor alerts about them. Also, Bitcoin has been criticized for its use in illegal transactions and lack of transparency. So, the Government of India as well governments of a few other countries have banned Bitcoin,' Shiv answered.

'Oh, is that so?'

'Yes. So, unless the government allows it, one can't really use Bitcoin as a currency. But currently, we can invest in cryptocurrencies as an asset even though we will have to pay a 30 per cent tax on any profits from the sale of cryptocurrencies,' Shiv continued.

'It is worth understanding the basics and keeping track of the developments regarding Bitcoin and other cryptocurrencies,' Siddharth replied. 'The regulations are still being debated. And like other central banks, the RBI is also likely to come out with its own digital currency.'

'Absolutely, let's do some research and discuss this again when we meet next time,' the group decided as they ended their discussion and got up to leave after having an excellent dinner.

Down the Rabbit Hole

The next week, Siddharth made his way to Bengaluru for an investment conference, where he was invited as a keynote speaker.

'Hi mamu,' Karan, his nephew, waved enthusiastically as Siddharth came out of the Bengaluru airport arrival gate on a Friday evening.

'Hey Karan, how are you doing? Good to see you,' Siddharth greeted his nephew and gave him a hug.

It had been a year since Karan had moved to Bengaluru to join a fintech start-up after his graduation.

'I am doing great. Nice to see you too. Mamu, these are my friends Dishant, Ajay and Mihir, whom I told you about earlier. We have been staying together here,' Karan introduced Siddharth to his flatmates.

'Yes, of course. Good to see you, guys,' Siddharth shook hands with them. 'Nice of you to have come all the way to the airport.'

'Ever since Karan told us about your first principle of financial planning, we have wanted to meet you,' Dishant told him.

'Oh, you mean Income – Savings = Expenses. Yes, once we understand that, our financial journey becomes easier,' Siddharth acknowledged with a smile.

'And once Karan told us about your second principle of financial planning, we were blown away,' Ajay continued.

'Of course. One who understands the compound interest formula, $V = P * (1 + r) \wedge t$, is set for life. Especially for young people like you who have time on their side, compound interest is the most powerful lever you will have in your life,' Siddharth was pleased to see that these youngsters were on the right track.

With that, he turned to Mihir, expecting him to add something to the discussion.

'You know, I am the joker in the pack,' Mihir told him. 'I haven't really adopted these principles yet.'

'Mihir is incorrigible,' Dishant said. 'He takes part in all our discussions but hasn't implemented any of your principles yet. He is living it up in Bengaluru.'

'Well, I don't think there is anything wrong in that,' Mihir responded quickly, 'I don't think in terms of saving pennies. I like to think big and have shared my views on what we should be doing. But, you guys are not up for it. You can't just keep playing like Rahul Dravid all the time. Sometimes you also need to play like Rishabh Pant.'

'Yes, but then you can get out quick too. Like what has happened with your latest adventure,' Dishant retorted.

'Okay, guys, Let's not start an argument at the airport,' Karan stepped in. 'We can discuss this over dinner.'

'Yes, even Siddharth is here. He can also provide us with some guidance,' Ajay seconded him.

'Sure,' Mihir said. 'I'd like to hear what Siddharth has to say on it too.'

'Okay, looks like you guys have something up your sleeves. That's interesting,' Siddharth said as they got into an Innova that the conference organizers had booked for him. 'So, what's the plan?'

'Well, it's already 8 p.m. So, we thought we'll head straight to dinner.' Karan was quick to respond.

'Sounds good, I hope you guys have picked a good restaurant. It's my treat,' said Siddharth as the Innova sped away from the airport. On the way, the boys spoke about their daily schedule, their jobs and life in Bengaluru.

'Okay. Here we are,' Mihir said as the vehicle came to a halt after an hour's drive and they got out. 'We thought you would like to enjoy some local cuisine. So, after much deliberation, we decided upon this restaurant as it is known for its authentic presentation of the finest creations from Karnataka, Andhra Pradesh, Telangana, Kerala, Pondicherry and Tamil Nadu.'

'This seems like an excellent choice. Let's go in,' Siddharth replied enthusiastically. He was famished as he had not eaten anything at Mumbai airport or on the plane.

The menu was indeed mouth-watering. For appetizers, they ordered majjigae (buttermilk), vadai (fritters), and vazhai shunti, which was described as 'golden dumplings of spiced raw banana hash, a speciality of Thanjavur' and seemed appetizing enough to try out.

'So Mihir, you mentioned that you would rather bat like Rishabh Pant and have some thoughts on what you guys should be doing,' Siddharth said as bit into a vadai. 'Let's have an open discussion.'

'Sure. See, what I have been telling these guys is that saving money and investing for the long term is good in terms of securing our financial future. But all that is going to take a long time,' Mihir replied.

'But you have time on your hands, right? What's the rush?' Siddharth asked him.

'Yes, but why wait twiddling our thumbs when we can take some action?'

'And what would that be? What do you want to do?'

'Invest in Bitcoin and other cryptocurrencies, of course. Actually, I have already done that. I have been encouraging these guys to do the same for some time now.'

'But since we knew that you were coming, we thought it was best to get your input on this before we took any decision,' Karan added.

'Oh okay, cryptocurrencies! I can see where this is going,' Siddharth smiled as he had a few gulps of buttermilk. 'I have been having quite a few of these conversations with my friends and clients too. You know, cryptocurrencies have been the most polarizing topic in the world of finance recently. Naysayers call it a bubble, while enthusiasts believe it holds the key to the future of finance. Tell me, have you guys done any research on Bitcoin and other cryptocurrencies?'

'Lots actually,' Dishant responded. 'And driven mainly by Mihir. It's tough to get him to do anything but if it's something he is interested in, then he goes hammer and tongs at it.'

'That's great. All four of you are computer science engineers. So, this is right up your alley from a technical perspective. I am curious to know what you have learnt. I have also done some research and spoken to a few knowledgeable people on this topic to get a hang of it but more from a finance and investment perspective. So, let's share what we know. Even I will get to learn something new from you youngsters.'

Takeaways

1. Bitcoin is a digital currency in which transactions are verified and records maintained by a distributed computer network called blockchain rather than by a centralized authority.

2. Although Bitcoin is banned in India and a few other countries, just like any currency, bitcoins can

be exchanged for other currencies, products and services.

3. Bitcoins use a combination of a public address and a private key. Losing one's private key would lead to loss of access to stored bitcoins.

4. Bitcoin is talked about as digital gold, i.e., a store of value than as a currency. But, Bitcoin prices themselves are quite volatile. And it has also not proven to be much of a hedge against rising inflation or geopolitical tensions.

18

Foundation for a New World: Blockchain

Decentralization using Blockchain Technology

'Okay. So, it all starts with the philosophy of decentralization supported by blockchain technology,' Mihir started.

'Hold on. What exactly do you mean by decentralization?' Siddharth interrupted him.

'Well, to start with, our monetary system is essentially a ledger—a record of who owns what. And when we buy or sell something, money moves by adding a new record to this ledger. Ledgers are important for our country's economy and even the global economy to work in a streamlined manner and hence they are all centralized currently. Banks, governments and monetary systems maintain these ledgers. Laws and sovereign forces protect these ledgers.'

'Okay. But how is that bad?'

'Somewhere, someone with some malicious intent can make unilateral changes in these ledgers and we can lose what we own. For example, someone can siphon off the money in our bank account without our knowledge. Else, they can forge papers and make changes in property ownership records without our knowledge and permission. Or the State can freeze our bank account or seize our assets. Many times, citizens have lost their money when these ledgers have been manipulated or destroyed—deliberately or otherwise.'

'Hmm. Normally, we never think of these things when operating our bank account or making investments. But this is an important point. So, where does blockchain fit in?'

'Blockchain technology enables us to build an autonomous system to manage these ledgers. With this technology at the base, it would be possible to build a robust decentralized finance system at a significantly lower cost and without the need for sovereign oversight. With blockchain, we can build a ledger to let people—in particular, people who don't trust one another—share valuable data in a secure, tamper-proof way. Essentially, it's a system for programmatic trust, which does not involve much human intervention.'

'Hmm. I understand the concept and can see how it can be useful. But from a technical perspective, I am the only one at this table who doesn't have a computer science background. So, can someone explain in plain English what a blockchain is?' Siddharth asked the group.

'Well, in simple terms, blockchain is just an interlinked chain of blocks of information stored on computers,' Karan responded. 'Each transaction is recorded in a data block. Transactions record things of interest—essentially entries that we would normally make in the ledger such as who, what, when, where, how much and any other data. Several transactions are grouped into a data block. Each block is encrypted. Each block is connected to the ones before and after it. These blocks form a chain that is linked securely together to prevent any block from being altered or a block being inserted between two existing blocks.'

'Understood. So, I can just imagine the blockchain to be like a normal chain of links except that in this case, the links are blocks of information. But how do we identify each block?'

'Each block has a unique identifier,' Karan explained. 'And blocks are linked back, each referring to the previous block in the chain. The sequence linking each block to the previous one creates a chain going back all the way to the first block ever created, known as the genesis block. A blockchain is just a piece of software code. So anyone can develop their own blockchain.'

'Okay. The description was easy enough to understand. But can you explain it with a simple practical example?'

'Sure. Let me give it a shot,' Ajay stepped in. 'Let's consider a simple example where A sells a digital piece of art to B for Rs 100. Then B sells it to C for Rs 250. And

C sells it to D for Rs 500. Each of these transactions represents a payment and a change in ownership.'

'Correct. Typically each of these would be a separate entry in a ledger.'

'Yes. In this case, each can be a new block in the blockchain. The first block will show that B made a payment to A and now owns the piece of art. It will have a unique identifier. The second block will show that C made a payment to B and now owns it. The second block will also have a unique identifier and it will be linked to the first block. Similarly, the third block will show that D made a payment to C and finally owns the piece of art. It will also have a unique identifier and will be linked to the second block. Now anyone can see the third block to identify who owns the piece of art, and because the blocks are in the form of an interlinked chain, they can also go back and see the history regarding who owned it in the past and what prices were paid. And the best part is it doesn't just have to be financial transactions.'

'Thanks, Ajay. You gave a very good example and I could visualize the blockchain. Can you give some other examples where blockchains are being used?'

'Sure. There are lots of them. For example, in the finance sector, blockchains are now being used in the asset management industry for trade processing and settlement and in the insurance industry for claims processing. They are also being used for cross-border payments and money lending. Other examples are blockchains used to store data from supply chain sensors, smart appliances, and our cars and smartphones. They are also being used to store healthcare data. And some countries have also started using blockchains for storing personal identification data, birth, wedding and death certificates, and passports. And, of course, they are used for storing cryptocurrencies and other digital assets.'

'Wow. I didn't realize blockchains were already so prevalent. But they sound just like another database, correct? What's so special about that? What's the big disruption blockchains are bringing about?'

'The key difference is that this database is shared or replicated across multiple computers or nodes,' Dishant clarified. 'A blockchain is decentralized and hence, there is no central place for it to be stored. It is stored in computers or systems all across the network.'

'Okay. So this is a completely different paradigm. Everything is distributed and decentralized.'

'You got it, mamu,' Karan was pleased. 'Essentially, no single node or entity controls the blockchain completely. So, there is higher transparency and nobody can make changes to the blockchain data unilaterally. This ensures that users are in control of their own information and transactions. So, in the example that Ajay mentioned regarding digital art, nobody can go in and unilaterally change the ownership of that piece of art. And when trust is critical but we can't trust everyone, blockchains are the solution.'

'Okay. I understand the value of the blockchain now,' Siddharth exclaimed. 'One of my clients recently got defrauded in a land transaction. He lives in Mumbai but owned some ancestral property in his native place in Karnataka. Without his knowledge, last year, his cousin sold off that property by forging the papers and bribing some corrupt officials there. He only came to know of it now and is running from pillar to post. These kinds of fraudulent transactions can be prevented by using blockchain technology, right?'

'You've hit the nail on the head,' Karan replied. 'By replicating the same information across multiple nodes and making it impossible to change past data, blockchains provide higher security. In your client's case, with blockchains, nobody would have been able to go in and change the ownership of his property without him being aware of it and giving his permission.'

'But how does blockchain technology ensure that?' Siddharth asked.

'Blockchain is highly secure and uses advanced cryptographic techniques and mathematical models of behaviour and decision-making. This makes it almost impossible to copy, manipulate or falsify data. Essentially, it's immutable,' Mihir jumped back into the discussion. 'And any update to the blockchain has to be validated.'

'Okay. And how does this validation process work?'

Mining

'Any update to the blockchain, in the form of the addition of new blocks of data, is called a transaction. A transaction is validated before the new block is added to the blockchain. The validation is done by people called "miners" and they get compensated with the cryptocurrency related to the blockchain, that is, Bitcoin, Ethereum, etc. This is called mining.'

'An example would be helpful, Mihir.'

'Sure. Let's go back to the example of digital art and try to keep things simple for ease of understanding. The last block will show that C had sold it to D for Rs 500. Now let's say D sells it to E for Rs 1000. The miner will validate that D owns that piece of art, E has made the payment to D and finally that E now owns the piece of art. Once this validation is done, the miner will add this new block to the blockchain.'

'And for this work, the miner gets compensated?'

'Yes, they get paid in the cryptocurrency which that particular blockchain uses, say Bitcoin, Ethereum, etc. This process is called mining because the miners are paid in cryptocurrency units which are newly created. The miners can sell those cryptocurrencies on exchanges for fiat currency or they can use them to buy goods and services. That's how new cryptocurrencies enter into circulation.'

'Got it. I have heard so much about Bitcoin mining but only understood it now. It's not that complicated to understand really.' Siddharth was quite pleased.

'Well then, it's a good jumping point into cryptocurrencies,' Mihir was excited to finally talk about the topic that he really wanted to discuss.

'Yes. But first, let's order the main course. Else, this discussion will keep going on,' Ajay said, laughing.

For the main course, they ordered sumptuous thalis and while they were waiting for them to arrive, they started their discussion on cryptocurrencies.

Takeaways

1. Blockchain is a distributed computer ledger which enables decentralization.
2. No single node or entity controls the blockchain completely. So, there is higher transparency and nobody can make changes to the blockchain data unilaterally.
3. Essentially, with blockchain, we can build a ledger to let people—in particular, people who don't trust one another—share valuable data in a secure, tamper-proof way. Essentially, it's a system for programmatic trust, which does not involve much human intervention.

CHAPTER 19

New Asset Class: Understanding Cryptocurrencies

Understanding the Basics of Cryptocurrencies

'In the blockchain ecosystem, any asset that is digitally transferable between two people is called a token,' Mihir started. 'These can be cryptocurrencies, non-fungible tokens or NFTs, or other types such as Decentralized Finance or DeFi tokens, governance tokens, security tokens, utility tokens, etc.'

'What's so special about tokens?' Siddharth was curious.

'With tokens, we can have programmable money.'

'What are you saying? Can you repeat that?'

'Yes. You see, in our day-to-day life, we use fiat money like rupees and dollars. These are examples of government-issued currency that is not backed by a physical commodity, such as gold or silver, but rather by the government that issued it. The value of fiat money is derived from the relationship between supply and demand, and the stability of the issuing government, rather than the worth of a commodity backing it. And fiat currency is not programmable.

'But cryptocurrency is programmable, which means we can build in any features we want. Currently, cryptocurrencies are primarily intended for use as a means of payment or money substitute. But they can have innovative features such as currency that can be used only for a specific purpose such as for buying food or which expires after a specified number of years. Currency tokens represent a decentralized alternative to traditional payment transactions and they are free of banks and central banks. The best-known currency token is Bitcoin.'

'Okay. Let's talk about Bitcoin in detail. I want to make sure I understand it completely.'

Bitcoin—From the Ground Up

'Bitcoin was invented by Satoshi Nakamoto. And no one knows who this person is. It seems to be a fictional name,' Mihir continued.

'Oh, really?' Siddharth was surprised.

'Yes. That adds to its mystique. Bitcoin is implemented using the blockchain. In a Bitcoin transaction, the following information is stored and transmitted: transaction date, amount sent, Bitcoin address of the sender and Bitcoin address of the receiver.'

'That's it! I guess it's kept light to make processing faster.'

'That's correct. Currently, Bitcoin has over 40,000 nodes in its network and processes over $30 billion in transactions each day, demonstrating that an application can be run in a distributed manner at scale, without compromising security.'

'Really! I wasn't aware that Bitcoin had reached this level of scale. What advantages does Bitcoin provide?'

'Essentially, Bitcoin is this very simple distributed computer ledger, which has three properties. First, it guarantees immutability—you cannot manipulate data that is committed on the blockchain. Second, it is set up as a shared public good. The code is open source and available to anyone. Third, it has censorship resistance. Anybody who wants to come in and use it can do so. Nobody can stop them. In this way, Bitcoin aims to provide decentralization, security and scalability.'

'Okay. Got it. And how many bitcoins are in existence?'

'As we discussed earlier, new bitcoins are mined, that is, created as the reward or incentive to the nodes for doing the work to keep the blockchain in good shape, ensure redundancy and maintain hygiene. The maximum number of bitcoins that can be issued, that is, mined, is 21 million by design.

'New bitcoins are added to the Bitcoin supply approximately every ten minutes, which is the average amount of time that it takes to create a new block of Bitcoin. By design, the number of bitcoins minted per block is reduced by 50 per cent after every 2,10,000 blocks, or about once every four years. As of September 2022, 19.1 million bitcoins have already been issued, with about 1.9 million bitcoins still to be released.'

'So, in the end, a total of 21 million bitcoins will be in existence?'

'Yes, the last bitcoin will be produced in 2140.'

'Got it. So, the supply of Bitcoin will be limited by design. But, Bitcoin is not the only cryptocurrency in existence, right?'

'You are right. There are almost 19,000 cryptocurrencies with a total market capitalization of almost $1 trillion.'

'Oh. That's too many cryptocurrencies!'

'Yes, most of them are not worth much. But the key ones are Bitcoin, Ethereum, Solana, Dogecoin, stablecoins, etc.'

'I have also heard about Ethereum. Let's talk about it next.'

Ethereum

'Ethereum is a general-purpose, programmable block-chain invented by Vitalik Buterin.' Dishant, who thought Ethereum was better than Bitcoin, jumped in.

'That sounds very ambitious, doesn't it?'

'It is. Vitalik's motivation was that in a blockchain we trust data because everyone has a copy of the data that is synced up to ensure that everything matches. So, he wanted to do the same not just with data but also with computation to build a trusted computer. Each one of us will run a copy of each one's computation and then we will sync it up to ensure that everything matches.'

'So, Bitcoin is a shared ledger. But Ethereum is a single-world computer. Is that right?'

'Yes. Ethereum attempts something "larger in scope" than Bitcoin. It is not just a distributed ledger, but something much more sophisticated. Ethereum is what we would call a "distributed state machine". It not only holds data on accounts or balances but holds an entire machine state. Ethereum uses smart contracts, which are coded programs that cover many different aspects of human agreement or at least simulate them. Hence, the underlying design of Ethereum is far more complex than Bitcoin.

'Okay. But what purpose does Ethereum really solve?'

'It was best explained by Naval Ravikant, who is a technologist and writer, that Ethereum enables a form of social scalability where it allows humans who don't know each other, who don't trust each other, who may never see each other again and don't even reveal their identities or locations to each other, to transact securely not just with money but with contracts, that is, any complex logic they can dream up that they can code up. They can do it through this very slow and very inefficient computer, but it removes all these layers of humans, bureaucrats and toll takers from the operation.'

'Hmm. So it solves the trust issue by removing all intermediaries. And we rely on programmatic trust.'

'Correct. And just like the Bitcoin blockchain has bitcoins as its currency, Ether (ETH) is the native cryptocurrency used on the Ethereum network and is used to compensate miners who secure transactions.'

'And like Bitcoin, is there a finite supply of Ethereum?'

'Absolutely. The total supply of ETH will be approximately 115 million.'

'And has Ethereum also scaled up like Bitcoin?'

'Yes. Ethereum has a wider scope. Several Ethereum-based financial products are already in existence. For example, Ethereum is used to send money around the globe, borrow funds with or without collateral, buy insurance, invest as part of a portfolio, etc. Real-time programmable money is a base building block for a lot of innovation and that opens up a wealth of new solutions to legacy problems. New banks, brokerages, insurance companies and more can potentially be built on crypto and blockchain platforms. Companies built on programmable money can be more transparent, trustworthy and efficient.'

'It looks like it will be important to monitor the developments in the Ethereum ecosystem. It could completely disrupt how we do almost everything. But, it doesn't mean that fiat currency is going to go away any time soon. Governments and central banks are not going to give up so easily, correct?'

'Absolutely. That's why we also have stablecoins and central bank digital currencies or CBDCs.'

'Okay. Let's discuss those next.'

Stablecoins

'A stablecoin is a cryptocurrency that is collateralized by the value of an underlying asset such as a fiat currency like the euro or the US dollar,' Karan explained. 'Stablecoins leverage the benefits of cryptocurrencies—such as transparency, security, immutability, digital wallets, fast transactions, low fees, privacy and programmability without losing the guarantees of trust and stability that come with using fiat currency or a collateralized asset.'

'What are some examples of stablecoins?'

'There are fiat-collateralized stablecoins such as USD Coin (USDC) and Tether, which are backed at a 1:1 ratio, meaning one stablecoin is equal to one unit of currency, like a dollar. So, for each stablecoin that exists, there is theoretically real fiat currency being held in a bank account to back it up. In addition, there are commodity collateralized stablecoins such as Digix Gold, crypto-collateralized stablecoins such as MakerDAO Dai, and non-collateralized stablecoins such as Basis.'

'Are the stablecoins true to their name? I've read about some controversies and pitfalls recently.'

'You are right. A stablecoin called Terra and its sister token Luna collapsed. They couldn't maintain their peg to the underlying fiat currency. The fact that a stablecoin with $18 billion in market capitalization collapsed highlights that even stablecoins are not exactly stable and that there is a lot of hype in this space.'

'Hmm. Looks like there are still some teething issues that need to be sorted out. You also mentioned CBDCs. What are they?'

Central Bank Digital Currency (CBDC)

'A CBDC represents the virtual form of a fiat currency,' Karan continued. 'It is an electronic record or a digital token. It is centralized, issued and regulated by a central bank and/or government authority of a country. Many central banks are doing pilots with CBDCs.'

'RBI is also doing a pilot, right?'

'Correct. RBI is evaluating various design considerations for its CBDC such as whether it should be a retail versus wholesale CBDC, which means, is the CBDC for use by the public or only for use by banks for interbank transactions, should it be based on distributed ledger technology or centralized, should it be token-based or account-based, should it be issued by RBI directly to the public or via banks, and how much anonymity will be allowed?'

'This was a good overview of some of the key cryptocurrencies. But, with so many cryptocurrencies in existence, how will we know which ones can succeed?'

'The traction that a cryptocurrency will achieve depends on the utility of the underlying project or of that token.'

'Yes. But, what is useful for you may not be useful for me, correct?'

'Absolutely. That's where subjectivity comes into the picture, making things difficult from an investment point of view. Only a handful of cryptocurrencies have managed to really scale up. But, we can also look at some parallels with fiat currency, such as the total supply of tokens of any particular cryptocurrency, how many tokens have been taken out of circulation, also called the burn, and how many are in circulation. This can give some indication of the traction achieved by that cryptocurrency and whether it stands a chance of becoming valuable in the future.'

'But as a lay person, how can I get a better understanding of these and other basic aspects of cryptocurrencies so that I have sufficient knowledge to even have a cogent discussion, forget about investing in crypto?'

'That will need some time and effort and a lot of reading. You will need to read whitepapers on each of the cryptocurrencies to understand the underlying technology they are using in terms of the software stack, programming language, and the consensus mechanism such as proof of stake or POS, proof of work or POW, or proof of history.

'You'll also need to understand the tokenomics in terms of how many tokens the founding team is keeping for themselves, how many are reserved for the community that is part of the underlying project, how many are transferred to the validators and how many are left for the public.

'The third aspect to understand is whether the cryptocurrency will be deflationary, that is, new tokens will be continuously mined in the future due to which their value can decline, or if it is inflationary, that is, mining of new tokens will stop at some point in the future and there will be a limited supply due to which their value can rise.

'Lastly, it is critical to do some diligence on the founders and the team. To see their track record, you will need to refer to their GitHub repository, see if the code is public or not, how many commits have been made by developers and whether there have been recent commits or not.'

'Hmm. It seems as though I will need to go through a lot of technical details if I really need to understand the potential for any cryptocurrency.'

'Yes. But an analogy is that if you want to invest in a stock, you do spend some time and effort to understand the business, evaluate the track record of the management team and analyse the financial statements and valuation, correct? This is no different. Else, you are just speculating.'

'Absolutely, if one wants to be a good investor, one has to put in the work irrespective of the asset class. So, I guess we have covered the basics of cryptocurrencies now?'

'Yes. But, we have just scratched the surface. One more concept you need to understand is DeFi.'

'DeFi? What exactly is it?'

Decentralized Finance (DeFi)

'Decentralized finance (DeFi) is a blockchain-based alternative financial ecosystem that does not rely on centralized financial intermediaries such as banks, brokerages and exchanges to offer financial products/ services,' Mihir explained.

'What does DeFi enable us to do?' Siddharth questioned him.

'DeFi enables users to transfer, trade, borrow and lend cryptocurrency, running on distributed blockchain-based infrastructure. The core concepts of DeFi— smart contract-linked decentralized applications— have enabled a host of financial applications, from borrowing and lending, staking the cryptocurrency that one holds to earn a yield or interest and the creation of decentralized exchanges. The users of the applications interact with each other in a peer-to-peer fashion relying primarily on "rule by code" rather than on any centralized intermediaries.'

'Okay. So, that's another interesting aspect to keep monitoring. The crypto space is indeed very fast-paced. But, tell me something, if someone wants to buy cryptocurrencies, where would they go and what process would they need to follow?'

'That's where crypto exchanges and wallets come into the picture.'

Takeaways

1. Cryptocurrencies are programmable money. They represent a decentralized alternative to traditional payment transactions that is free of banks and central banks.
2. Bitcoin is the best-known cryptocurrency. It is a very simple distributed computer ledger, which has three properties—immutability, publicly sharing and censorship resistance.
3. Ethereum is a general-purpose, programmable blockchain, which can remove all intermediaries from a transaction.
4. New banks, brokerages, insurance companies and more can potentially be built on crypto and blockchain platforms. Companies built on programmable money can be more transparent, trustworthy and efficient.

20

How Do I Do It? Crypto Exchanges, Regulations, Valuation

Crypto Exchanges and Wallets

'We can open an account at a crypto exchange, which is a marketplace where we can buy and sell cryptocurrencies, such as Bitcoin, Ether or Dogecoin, etc.' Mihir continued. 'Cryptocurrency exchanges work a lot like other trading platforms that we are familiar with, such as stock trading. They provide you with accounts where you can create different order types to buy, sell and speculate in the crypto market.'

'Can you give some examples?'

'Sure. A decentralized exchange or DEX, such as Oasis.app or Uniswap, allows for direct peer-to-peer cryptocurrency transactions. Whereas a centralized exchange or CEX, such as Coinbase or Binance, is controlled by a third party, which has control of user funds. Overall, there are nearly 600 cryptocurrency exchanges worldwide enabling investors to trade Bitcoin, Ethereum and other digital assets. But costs, quality and safety vary widely and some exchanges have been victims of fraud wherein someone siphoned off their cryptocurrencies, while a few have gone bankrupt. There are a number of crypto exchanges in India too. But due to onerous government regulations, they are in the process of getting acquired, closing down or shifting to other countries.'

'Okay. I understood what crypto exchanges are. But where would one keep their cryptocurrency?'

'Cryptocurrencies are held in wallets. These can be hot wallets or cold wallets.'

'What exactly are these wallets?'

'Hot wallets are based online. They include web-based wallets, mobile wallets or exchange wallets, which online cryptocurrency exchanges typically offer. They are always online and easily accessible using a web browser or mobile device. Most consumer-friendly digital asset exchanges offer some combination of hot and/or cold wallet storage solutions. Popular hot wallets include Trust Wallet or MetaMask. An analogy is our Paytm wallet, Ola wallet or FASTag wallet where we store some cash in digital form, which we can then spend when needed without having to use physical cash.'

'And cold wallets?'

'Cold wallets are offline. They include hardware wallets, cold storage or offline storage, which are physical wallets that "hold" crypto offline. In many scenarios, cold wallets offer superior security compared to hot wallets, as private keys and other sensitive information is stored offline. However, cold wallets can be misplaced due to user error, theft or damage beyond repair. Cold wallet solutions range from incredibly sophisticated wallets held in secure vaults to high-quality consumer-grade hardware wallets to "paper wallets" that simply consist of a quick response or QR code or alphanumeric strings printed or written on paper.'

'I have heard of cases where people have forgotten their private keys or misplaced their USB drives where they had stored their cryptocurrencies.'

'Yes, one has to be very careful in that regard.'

'Okay. In simple terms, the steps I have to follow are first, I have to open an online wallet and a crypto exchange account after doing my Know Your Customer, that's KYC, and connect the two. Second, I need to buy some cryptocurrency on an exchange using fiat currency like rupees or dollars from my regular bank account. And third, I can transfer the cryptocurrency to my online wallet.'

'Correct.'

'Then, if I want to transact using my cryptocurrency, say I want to buy something from you, all I need to do is to transfer the cryptocurrency from my wallet to your wallet.'

'Right.'

'Lastly, if I want to sell my cryptocurrency, I just sell it on the crypto exchange, get proceeds in fiat currency and transfer it to my bank account.'

'You got it.'

'This process is quite streamlined. No wonder so many people in India started speculating in crypto in a short span of time.'

'Yes. And it was not just in the metros and tier I cities. Many people from tier II and tier III towns, and some of the rural areas too got into crypto trading.'

Regulations regarding Cryptocurrencies

'We've spoken mostly about the advantages of cryptocurrencies so far. Aren't there a lot of concerns too, because of which they have been in the news?' Siddharth asked, wanting to explore all aspects and get a balanced view.

'You are right,' Ajay replied. 'Wallets and blockchains provide anonymity. Hence, there have been concerns regarding anti-money laundering, KYC regulation violations, financing of terrorism and drugs, stability of individual financial institutions and the entire global financial system, as well as tax evasion.'

'I guess that's why governments are keen to bring in strict regulations for cryptocurrencies and introduce CBDCs as soon as possible. The Indian government has banned Bitcoin and other cryptocurrencies. They want to prevent people from sending money outside the country illegally using crypto. So they have introduced tax deducted at source (TDS) on crypto transactions so that they can track users and take action if needed.

'But, instead of going for a blanket ban, some other countries such as Australia are planning to decide which cryptocurrencies to allow based on who is issuing that token. The US is working on establishing a regulatory framework to allow banks to facilitate ownership of crypto assets for customers and a few other countries are also evaluating that option. In a sense, they are taking a more inclusive approach than countries like India and China.

'Another issue is that cryptocurrency mining also consumes a lot of electricity, which in many countries, including India, is still generated in a big way using coal. So, it is not seen to be good for the environment.'

'Clearly, the government does not want the masses to get involved too much in cryptocurrencies.'

Valuing Cryptocurrencies

'Okay. Now that we have talked a lot about this topic, let's come to the key question. How are cryptocurrencies valued?' Siddharth asked them.

'We don't have a clue. We were really hoping you would help us understand that,' Mihir shrugged.

'The way I look at it, as an asset class, cryptocurrencies are best understood by comparing them to gold. Bitcoin has even been referred to as "digital gold". Gold is considered a store of value and hence is seen as a hedge against inflation and geopolitical tensions. Gold prices move up during periods of high inflation or war or some other crisis. However, they are negatively impacted by rising interest rates and the strengthening US dollar. In addition, demand for gold by consumers, central banks and gold ETFs and the corresponding supply from gold miners also impacts its price. Overall, it's not possible to calculate an intrinsic value for gold as it doesn't generate any cash flows.'

'Understood. And how about crypto?'

'Well, so far, cryptocurrencies have not really proved to be a good hedge against inflation, recession or geopolitical conflict. Hence, they can't really be considered to be a store of value.'

'But cryptocurrencies have been used in cases where some countries have raised funds through crowdsourcing and in other cases where some ultra-high-net-worth individuals have converted their assets to cryptocurrencies to prevent them from getting confiscated by their government.'

'Yes, that's right. Also, cryptocurrencies have turned out to be what we would call a high beta asset class and are highly correlated to high-growth tech stocks. It means that their price moves up and down following stock prices of tech stocks but they are much more volatile. We have seen that as interest rates are rising, valuations of high-growth tech stocks have corrected and cryptocurrency valuations are also following the same trend.'

'No wonder Bitcoin prices have crashed by more than 70 per cent!'

'The key point is that, just like gold, there is no way to fundamentally value cryptocurrencies as they don't provide any cash flows. Their value depends on the network effect and scarcity value, that is, supply and demand. Essentially it's driven by what you think someone else will think it will be worth in the future.'

'So in that sense, it's speculation and not investment.'

'Exactly. In addition, earlier, interest rates were low. So, people would have preferred to speculate on cryptocurrencies rather than keep money in their bank accounts. But now that interest rates are rising, people may prefer to keep money in the bank than speculate in cryptocurrencies.'

'Oh, okay. Looks like we really need to think carefully before speculating on cryptocurrencies,' Mihir exclaimed.

'Yes. And it's important to keep the taxation angle also in mind.'

'Could you please explain that? We are not so clear about that aspect,' Karan replied.

'In India, the Union Budget 2022 had proposed taxing crypto assets at 30 per cent, effective 1 April 2022. In addition, the honourable finance minister has introduced an amendment clarifying that no tax deduction or set-off would be available in place of mining cost of crypto assets and other virtual digital assets or VDAs, or losses from their transfer. Effectively, trading in VDAs, including cryptocurrencies and non-fungible tokens or NFTs, is being treated as a speculative activity like buying lottery tickets and is being taxed accordingly.

'In addition, the government plans to impose GST, the goods and service tax, of 18 per cent on all VDA transactions. These transactions will also attract TDS of 1 per cent.'

'Essentially, it will not be that attractive to speculate in cryptocurrencies.'

'Yes. The government doesn't want the masses indulging in this activity,' Siddharth said with a smile.

'But, from what I have read, even stock markets across the world used to see a lot of speculation and scams in the initial years, correct?' Mihir said with some thought.

'You are absolutely right,' Siddharth responded. 'But over time, the government introduced regulations and processes got digitized and streamlined as well. Investing in the stock market became safer for investors and the government could also track their investments.'

'Now, stock markets have created a lot of wealth for people. We may see the same happening with crypto too,' Mihir sounded hopeful.'

'I guess we are still at a nascent stage as far as Crypto is concerned,' Siddharth said. 'It's just like the Internet in the 1990s when some people thought it would revolutionize the world, which it did, while others thought it would have limited use. So, we'll have to wait and see. Even the government and central banks across the world are still trying to figure things out as far as cryptocurrencies are concerned.'

HODLING

'Another risk is that cryptocurrencies are very volatile, right?' Siddharth continued. 'I have heard the term

HODL in that regard. What exactly does that mean?' Siddharth asked.

'Today, HODL has two popular definitions,' Karan explained. 'First, it is a misspelling of the word hold, used in reference to holding cryptocurrencies.'

'And, second?'

'As an acronym for "Hold On for Dear Life", also used in reference to holding cryptocurrencies, which are extremely volatile. HODL first appeared on the Bitcoin talk forums in 2013, when user Game Kyuubi created a thread titled "I AM HODLING". In the thread, Game Kyuubi lamented their poor trading skills before vowing to keep holding while ignoring market movements. And since then, many people who have been speculating in cryptocurrencies have adopted that term.'

'Why don't you tell Siddharth that you have also become a HODLER?' Dishant joked, referring to Mihir.

'That's true. I had bought some bitcoins at low prices earlier and made good money on them. But in that excitement, I proceeded to buy some more bitcoins when they went above $50,000. Of course, we can buy fractional bitcoins. So, I only ended up investing a few lakh rupees, which I had borrowed from my dad.'

'And what happened after that?'

'Well, Bitcoin prices rose to a high of $69,000 and I was elated. But I didn't sell. And after that, Bitcoin crashed to less than $20,000. I sold some of my bitcoins along the way but am still holding a big chunk. So I have become a HODLER after suffering a significant loss. But mind you, I am a believer.'

'That happens to a lot of people in the stock market too. But Bitcoin is in another league,' Siddharth laughed. 'Going back to what you said at the beginning, speculating in cryptocurrencies would be batting like Rishabh Pant in the early stages of his career.'

'You are absolutely right. But he seems to have cracked the code and found a method to his madness. He still lives and dies by the sword. But he is certainly showing more maturity when it comes to choosing the right bowler and right deliveries to play his shots.'

'So, in the same way, we should also find a method to the madness in cryptocurrencies and not blindly rush in by speculating recklessly.'

'So, what's the best way then?'

'The answer lies in asset allocation.'

'Could you please explain in a little more detail?'

'As I keep on telling my clients, apart from some emergency funds, we should make sure the core of our investment portfolio is in asset classes such as domestic stocks, international stocks, bonds, gold and real estate. If at all we are interested in cryptocurrencies, then let's be clear that it's speculation and not an investment. Accordingly, we should only allocate a small portion, say 2–3 per cent, of our overall portfolio to cryptocurrencies, if at all, and be prepared for the higher volatility. It would not be prudent to make it a part of the core portfolio.'

'Okay, Siddharth. I understand what you are saying and will keep that in mind. I won't be so reckless going forward,' Mihir promised as they got up to leave.

Takeaways

1. Similar to gold, it is not possible to assign any intrinsic value to Bitcoin and other cryptocurrencies as they don't generate any cash flows. Prices can be highly volatile as they are just a function of supply and demand.

2. One can trade Bitcoin and other cryptocurrencies by opening an online wallet and an account on a crypto exchange.

3. However, the governments of India and a few other countries have banned cryptocurrencies and are introducing strict regulations on crypto exchanges as wallets and blockchains provide anonymity due to which there have been concerns regarding violations of anti-money laundering and KYC regulations.

4. To discourage speculation, capital gains tax on virtual digital assets, including cryptocurrencies, has been set at 30 per cent, similar to lottery tickets. Losses from transactions cannot be used to set off profits from other transactions.

21

Upcoming Asset Class: NFTs

The next day, after finishing his conference session, Siddharth met with his IIT Bombay classmates, Srini and Anand. Srini had come down from the US and they had decided to catch up that evening at Anand's home in Koramangala, Bengaluru.

'You know, yesterday I met with my nephew and his flatmates here. They are all computer science engineers and I got a good grounding on blockchain and cryptocurrencies,' Siddharth said, as he gave them a lowdown on his insights from the discussion.

'Yes, Siddharth. Cryptocurrencies are quite popular in the US too and many people are working on innovative solutions using blockchain technology,' Srini told him. He was working at a tech start-up in Silicon Valley and seemed to be clued into the latest developments in the world of blockchain and crypto. 'NFTs are one such innovation. I am sure you must have heard about them.'

'Of course,' Siddharth replied. 'Let's talk about NFTs. That's a topic which many of my clients, especially millennials, are interested in nowadays. So, I have a lot of questions.'

'Actually, I have also bought some NFTs just for the bragging rights,' Srini replied with a smile.

'Good for you. So, tell us more!' Both Siddharth and Anand goaded him on.

Non-fungible Tokens (NFTs)

'It would be good to start with some examples,' Srini continued. 'Do you know that CryptoKitties, CryptoPunks and Bored Ape NFTs have become popular and some of them have sold for $2,00,000 to $3,00,000?'

'Yes. I had read about it. It sounds incredible,' Siddharth replied.

'Yes, many celebrities bought them as cute collectibles and for social media bragging rights as well as for signalling that they are part of an elite community. Internationally, celebrities like Snoop Dogg and Lindsay Lohan have released unique memories, artwork and moments as securitized NFTs,' Srini continued.

'And in India, Amitabh Bachchan auctioned the Madhushala NFT—a collection of poems written by his father and recorded in the superstar's own voice, right?' Siddharth replied.

'It looks like you are quite up to speed on NFTs,' Anand exclaimed.

'Well, my clients keep me on my toes.'

'That's good to know. However, we are still at a nascent stage in terms of the evolution of NFTs and a majority of NFTs are not worth much,' Srini clarified.

'Yes, but it would still be good to get a basic understanding of this topic.'

'Absolutely. First of all, an NFT is a virtual digital asset. It's different from a tangible asset like a house, car or a painting.'

'Okay. So, we can only see an NFT on our laptop or mobile but cannot touch and feel it.'

'Correct. An NFT is also different from a traditional digital asset like an image or video. It's a crypto token or a crypto asset. But it's different from a cryptocurrency like Bitcoin, Ethereum or stablecoins.'

'How exactly is it different from a cryptocurrency?'

'It's different because an NFT is a non-fungible asset.'

'Can you explain with an example?'

'A simple example of a fungible asset is cash which we use in our everyday life. One Rs 500 note is the same as any other Rs 500 note. Further, I can give you a Rs 500 note and you can give me five 100-rupee notes back as they have the same value. In the same way, one bitcoin is the same as any other bitcoin. In contrast, one NFT cannot be replaced with another and it cannot be sub-divided.'

'Okay. Got it. But then, how is the value of an NFT decided?'

'The value of each NFT may be different based on the value of the underlying unique asset and its scarcity value, that is, how many copies of the underlying asset are in circulation. And that is something which the creator of the asset decides.'

'Hmm. That's interesting. I guess the Bored Ape NFTs are selling for hundreds of thousands of dollars as celebrities are using them for signalling that they are part of an elite community but the rest of the NFTs are not worth much.'

'You've got that right.'

'Can you briefly explain how an NFT works technically, but in simple language?' Anand asked Srini.

'Sure. An NFT is a unique digital asset whose ownership is tracked on a blockchain. It can be digital goods, artwork, virtual land or real estate, collectable cards, etc. In practice, an NFT is simply a unique token representing a digital file. Each token has a canonical identifier, which is a unique ID.'

'Okay. And that file has additional information about the digital asset?'

'Exactly. Hooked to the NFT's identifier is arbitrary metadata; for example, who created it, what it's about or its price history. Essentially, we can define ownership in a file and upload that on a blockchain, which then guarantees the provenance and attribution.'

'How exactly does an NFT work?

Minting NFTs

'When an NFT is minted, that is, newly created by a creator, this information is immutably registered on the blockchain and becomes the digital passport for the work. Digital scarcity is created as every instance is unique and differentiated. Creators can program how the value of the NFTs must be shared using smart contracts.'

'That's a new term. What do you mean by smart contracts?'

'Artists can program in royalties as smart contracts in NFTs. Royalties give the creator a percentage of the sale price each time the NFT is sold on a marketplace. This is an attractive feature as artists generally do not receive future proceeds after their art is first sold. NFT royalty payments are perpetual and are executed by smart contracts automatically even on secondary sales. With most marketplaces, the creator can choose their royalty percentage. 5 to 10 per cent is considered a standard royalty.'

'But there are so many marketplaces where NFTs can be bought and sold. Do NFTs work across all of them?'

'Absolutely. NFTs are composable. There are open protocols that can plug into each other. NFT protocols allow them to be traded with anyone in the world. This allows us to use an NFT across different systems and platforms.'

'Okay. But is something valuable just because it's an NFT?'

'Well, when someone buys an NFT, they're not buying the actual digital artwork; they're buying a link to it. And worse, they're buying a link that, in many cases, lives on the website of a new start-up that could fail within a few years. Decades from now, how will anyone verify whether the linked artwork is the original? So, that risk is there with NFTs.'

'This was excellent, Srini. You have given us a good grounding on the basics of NFTs. But is there really a practical use for NFTs?' Anand asked him.

NFTs in real life

'We can broadly split the use of NFTs into two basic approaches—those with utility and those primarily used as collectibles, and some as a combination of the two.'

'That's interesting.'

'Utility-centred NFTs usually open up access to exclusive events and are starting to be used by consumer brands for creating marketing buzz or improving loyalty points; they are also used to capture a "deed of ownership" of real-world assets.'

'Okay. And the collectibles?'

'Collectibles are usually seen as speculative investments. CryptoArt enthusiasts and investors tend to judge NFTs not by traditional art standards, but by characteristics such as "dankness", which captures the potency of expression and creativity, and usually indicates an exceptionally rare image gone viral. This helps explain why pictures of bored apes or pudgy penguins are trading for millions of dollars.'

'Which of the two types are more popular?'

'The most popular use cases of NFTs today span gaming—by volume of transactions—and art, by the value of transactions. But we are seeing increasingly new use cases across other domains too. Today, there are close to ten different types of NFTs ranging across music, art, game objects, access and identity.'

'And, how do NFTs help content creators?'

Advantages of NFTs for Creators and Artists

'Normally, when we share some content, such as a photo, video or podcast on a platform, the platform gets to decide how to monetize it. They may share some of the proceeds with us, but that is their prerogative. Normally they keep the lion's share. That's where NFTs come in.'

'So, NFTs enable artists and content creators to monetize their creations in a better way?'

'Correct. For example, artists no longer have to rely on galleries or auction houses to sell their art. And content creators won't need to depend on platforms to share their content. Instead, the artist or content creator can sell their creation directly to the consumer as an NFT, which also lets them keep more of the profits.'

'I guess this is related to our earlier discussion on smart contracts?'

'Absolutely. NFTs can include smart contracts as part of creating the NFT. Platforms will enforce the smart contract every time a transaction is executed.'

'Okay. Understood. So, tell me, as a consumer, what exactly am I getting when I buy an NFT?'

NFT from a Consumer Standpoint

'From a buyer's point of view, we get our own unique copy of the original asset. We can think of it as our own copy of an image, poem, song or video. NFTs are like certificates of authenticity for digital things versus physical things. They prove you are the owner. And as I mentioned earlier, the value of the NFT will depend on the underlying asset and how many copies are available in the market.'

'Are there any downsides to NFTs that we should be aware of?'

'While NFTs are useful to mark and verify authenticity once it has been recorded on the blockchain, today's NFT ecosystem makes it very easy to start off with a work that belongs to someone else and mint that on the blockchain as an NFT. While there is an immutable on-chain record that points to a specific piece of work, that piece of work itself could easily be counterfeited to begin with.'

'So, its validity could be void from the initial point itself and we wouldn't even know about it?'

'That's right. Another term you may hear is "rug pulling". In crypto parlance, this is when creators of a project hype it up and then suddenly stop backing the project and disappear from the ecosystem. This results in the price of the NFT falling steeply, leading to massive losses for unsuspecting buyers and investors who already have a stake in the projects. Although not restricted to NFTs, rug pull scams are reported to have stolen crypto assets worth billions of dollars.'

'That's too bad.'

'Another aspect to keep in mind is "wash trading", which refers to executing a transaction in which the same person or entity is on both sides of the trade. Wash trading provides a misleading picture of liquidity and sale price, as all this information is captured on the blockchain.'

'So, a casual NFT buyer could believe that the history of transactions provides proof of the value of the NFT they are buying whereas the underlying data would be manipulated. This happens in penny stocks in the stock market too.'

'Lastly, most NFTs do not store the data on-chain as it would be too expensive. Instead, they only contain a URL that points to the data. And anyone with access to the underlying URL could easily swap out the base file.'

'So, there is nothing in the NFT specification itself that restricts where the underlying piece of work "should" be, or even allows us to confirm whether something is the "correct" piece of work?'

'Correct. Although there are these negative aspects about NFTs, the good part is that, notwithstanding the hype cycle and astronomical valuations around NFTs, most transactions tend to be for a small value currently.'

'And where can one buy these NFTs?'

'There are a number of online exchanges, such as OpenSea, where NFTs are traded. So, one can buy and sell NFTs there.'

Investing in NFTs

'Okay. This was a very helpful overview of NFTs. But, from an investor's point of view, it's also important to understand the tax implications of investing in NFTs. So if you are interested, I can talk about it,' Siddharth said.

'Yes, please do. We don't have any inkling of that.'

'The Indian Union Budget 2022 had proposed taxing VDAs at 30 per cent effective 1 April 2022. As of now, in India, the finance minister has introduced an amendment clarifying that no tax deduction or set-off would be available in place of losses from their transfer. Effectively, trading in VDAs, including NFTs, is being treated as a speculative activity, akin to buying lottery tickets.'

'Oh, we were not aware of that. I guess it will take some time before NFTs become a mainstream investment avenue in India then.'

'Yes. You are right. But it's an interesting area to monitor as it can unleash a wave of creativity since content owners will be able to monetize their work more efficiently.'

'Absolutely. But, there is an even more interesting area that I am working on now at my start-up,' Srini said with a smile.

'Oh, really. What is it?' both Siddharth and Anand asked in unison.

'You know that Mark Zuckerberg changed the name of Facebook to Meta, right?'

'Yes.'

'Do you know why?'

'Because he is reorienting the company to focus on something called the metaverse.'

'You are right. And that's what we are also working on at our start-up.'

'Oh, really? Then it's good that we met you today. Do tell us more about it.'

'Yes, But let's have dinner first,' Anand told them. 'We can continue our discussion afterwards.'

Takeaways

1. An NFT is a unique digital asset whose ownership is tracked on a blockchain. It can be digital goods, artwork, virtual land or real estate, collectable cards, etc.
2. Creators and artists can program in royalties as smart contracts in NFTs so that they get a royalty not just on the initial sales but on secondary sales as well, in perpetuity.
3. Utility-centred NFTs usually open up access to exclusive events whereas collectible NFTs are speculative investments.
4. From a buyer's point of view, we get our own unique copy of the original asset. We can think of it as our own copy of an image, poem, song or video. NFTs are like certificates of authenticity for digital things versus physical things. They prove you are the owner.
5. There are a number of online exchanges, such as OpenSea, where NFTs are traded.

22

A Virtual World:
The Metaverse

A Virtual World

'To put it simply, the metaverse is the next iteration of the Internet that combines our digital and physical lives. It is a computer-generated world where you can meet people, attend classes or training sessions, play games, watch concerts, do your job, visit places, browse store shelves, etc.,' Srini started after dinner.

'So, it is a digital world inhabited by digital representations of people and things?'

'Exactly. The easiest way to think about the metaverse is how Mark Zuckerberg described it, as really just Internet+, which means you can think of it as Internet + 3D, Internet + persistence, Internet + VR/AR.'

'Really? So anyone will be able to be a part of it?'

'Yes. The metaverse is a shared virtual world that people access from the Internet. This virtual world is an extension or a parallel overlay to the real world. It brings together NFTs and crypto. You can buy virtual land to personalize your own space, buy collectibles, interact with others and attend events.'

'My wife keeps complaining that we can't afford to buy land here in Bengaluru now. I might as well buy a plot in the metaverse,' Anand joked.

'What would you say are the key characteristics of the metaverse?' Siddharth asked Srini.

'There are a few key elements to consider,' Srini continued. 'The first element is immersion. Virtual environments will be more immersive, which means they will allow the user to live the experience instead of just observing it on their computer or mobile screen. Users can also port themselves seamlessly from one experience to another.

'The second is the social element. Imagine being in a place where you can interact and socialize, not only with a small group of your friends but also with thousands and potentially millions of people in one virtual set-up. Imagine going to a concert where you can be with millions of people.

'The third element is expressiveness. Users in the real-time 3D worlds are represented by avatars, allowing you to express yourself in completely new ways that you may not want to express in real life. For example, in the metaverse, I can be whomever I want and wear whatever

I want—things that I may not be comfortable wearing in the real world.

'The fourth element is real-time interactivity. Your actions in the real world would be mimicked by your avatar in the metaverse instantly. You would be able to interact with another person's avatar in the same way that you would interact with them physically in the real world.'

Online Avatars

'So, whatever I am doing in the real world, I will be able to do in the metaverse. And I can even have multiple avatars or identities, allowing me to express myself in more creative ways. Is that right?'

'Absolutely. People are likely to have multiple identities in the metaverse—maybe as many as ten avatars per person—for example, one for sports activities or games, another for school or work, another for music concerts.'

'That makes sense. Most of us already have multiple identities. We are not the same person at home with family as we are with office colleagues or school friends. We often have different attitudes, personalities and identities depending on the environment around us.'

'Also, technology enables us to do things virtually in a more seamless and frictionless manner. It allows us to creatively express our personalities, such as dressing up for a wedding, sports event, or work. We already do most of this today in our real life, but the way this will be manifested in the metaverse will be totally different.'

'So, similar to the material possessions we have in our real life, such as a house, vehicle, clothes, accessories, etc., we'll have to buy them in the metaverse too, correct?'

'Right. Digital property in the metaverse will likely span skins, avatars, emotes, NFTs, fungible tokens and collectibles, among others. One way to visualize these is as virtual items stored in a digital wallet or "digital closet" that one can move in the metaverse.'

'I can see where this is going. It's going to be double spending for us—in the real world and also in the metaverse,' Siddharth pointed out.

'We could have two, five or even ten avatars for distinct purposes within our personality and we are likely to treat or invest in each one of them differently. But this transformation is likely to first occur with the younger demographic population as they are more likely to experiment,' Srini clarified.

'So, are you saying that our spending could more than double also given that we will have multiple avatars? Especially, our kids are going to be spending a lot more than what they do now? No wonder you are working on a start-up related to the metaverse.'

'We may reach a point of time where human beings will potentially consider their virtual presence or avatars to be as valuable, if not more, than their physical or real-life identity. It isn't unimaginable to think of us making significant investments in the digital presence of our avatars. This could translate to significant market potential for commerce, fashion, sports and gaming. In such a scenario, the potential market size of the metaverse could be over trillions of dollars. That's what made it attractive for us.'

'This is all in the future, correct? Is the metaverse seeing any traction from consumers currently?'

'Yes. Actually, the metaverse seems to have appeal across gender, geographies and age groups as it is redefining socializing and communication.

'The metaverse is expected to be a significant part of our everyday lives. And consumers are excited about new ways to connect with people, explore digital worlds, meet with remote colleagues and collaborate with them. And I am not referring just to Gen Z but the millennials as well as teenagers too. And we are seeing increasing interest not just in developing countries such as the US but in emerging countries in Asia too.

'Also, consumers are open to spending money on digital assets now. They are interested in new technologies and experiences, and that is driving significant investment in this space.'

'That's good to know. So far, we have looked at the metaverse from a consumer's point of view. But I read that corporates are also looking to make their mark early on in the metaverse. Can you give some concrete examples of what some companies are already doing or planning to do in the metaverse?'

The Metaverse for Corporates and Brands

'Sure. There are a host of metaverse-related initial experiments going on in areas such as commerce, art, media, advertising, healthcare and social collaboration. It is being used as a gaming platform, as a virtual retail destination, as a training tool and as an advertising channel currently.'

'There seems to be a wide variety of applications for corporates to consider. No wonder there is increasing interest in this space.'

'Yes. Brands like Nike, Gucci, Ralph Lauren and others are especially keen to move fast and build their presence in the metaverse. For them, it provides a new avenue for customer engagement, creating brand awareness and building communities and virtual showrooms, which can lead to commerce and the sale of virtual goods.

'On the enterprise side, we are likely to see the growth of enterprise software as several industries are keen to experiment with the metaverse and build industrial applications and digital twins that would enable them to run simulations of various scenarios and help in developing their business plans. Many companies like BMW and NewSky are experimenting with the metaverse for product demos, creating virtual workspaces and immersive training, and organizing virtual conferences, tradeshows and business-to-business or B2B events. They have also tried to conduct client meetings to increase their client engagement.'

'Oh, is that so? I was not aware of these developments at all. That's really interesting.'

'In the coming years, we should see applications in internal company collaboration, customer service, sales and marketing, targeted advertising, events and conferences, engineering and design, and workforce training, among other activities. The retail and fashion sectors should see a lot of innovation. In healthcare, telemedicine and delivery of services outside large hubs should improve.'

'But which ones are likely to come first?'

'Over the next five years, we should see online gaming being redefined using the metaverse. Additionally, more applications are likely to emerge around socialization, for events such as fashion shows, music concerts and sports events. We are already seeing social tokens, which give permissioned access to gated private communities or to creators offering incentives to fans. In general, social tokens align participants behind a collective mission related to the community or the creator.

'We are also likely to see a consistent growth of metaverse commerce with users spending money to purchase NFTs or digital items for their avatars. Consumption of virtual goods is likely to grow.

'We should also see the evolution of real-world NFTs, which are a way of establishing a bridge connecting the metaverse world and its NFTs with real-world assets. It is a way to tokenize physical property so that it can be uniquely identified in the digital realm, traded, governed and owned using the same underlying technology that is driving the crypto economy. For example, ownership of a physical building can be split into smaller parts and their NFTs can then be sold and traded in the metaverse.'

Infrastructure for the Metaverse

'But is all of this even possible with the current back-end infrastructure? Won't that take a long time to set up?'

'Think about the convergence of virtual, augmented and mixed reality, spatial computing, 5G+ speeds and reimagined human-computer interaction. That's the territory we're talking about when we say metaverse and there is tremendous innovation happening in these segments. A device-agnostic metaverse would be accessible via personal computers, game consoles and smartphones, resulting in a large ecosystem.'

'But how did this even start?'

'The metaverse as a concept has been around for a few decades. However, interest in the virtual world spiked at the end of 2021, following a rise in sales of NFTs as well as announcements from the large tech companies indicating their interest and investment in the space.'

'But, taking it to the next level is going to require a lot of investment, correct?'

'Yes, the content streaming environment of the metaverse will likely require a computational efficiency improvement of over 1000 times of today's levels. Investment will be needed in areas such as computational resources, storage, network infrastructure, consumer interface hardware and game development platforms. We also need to create an ecosystem that enables developers and content creators to collaborate easily and share their creativity.'

'So, the next few years will be ones of experimentation, adventure, trial and error, right?'

'Yes. We also need to keep in mind that for customers to be able to access more advanced devices, we need to see an increase in purchasing power. Also, many of us may buy virtual reality or VR headsets for their novelty. But will we use them regularly when it's not clear what impact they could have on our health and well-being? Will we get close to using augmented reality or AR, or VR devices for as many hours as our mobile phones? These are questions to which we don't have answers yet.'

'It seems like it will be a very different environment, to be honest.'

'Yes. The definition of what counts as money in the open metaverse is also likely to be very different from what counts as money in the real world today.'

'So, what you are saying is that real-world currency won't work in the metaverse and it will all be based on cryptocurrency?'

'Interoperability and seamless exchange between underlying blockchain technology are critical to ensure a frictionless user experience in the metaverse. Different forms of cryptocurrency are expected to dominate but given that there are multiple blockchains in the crypto ecosystem, cryptocurrency will likely coexist with fiat currencies, CBDCs and stablecoins.'

'So, from what I understood, in the metaverse, value will be transferred in tokenized format—in the form of crypto, CBDCs or stablecoins—and ownership would be registered by NFTs or similar blockchain-based digital assets.'

'Exactly. It would be a big change from the current monetary and financial world.'

'Isn't there a threat of regulations given the increased focus on cryptocurrencies?'

'You are right. If the metaverse is indeed the new iteration of the Internet, it will most likely attract greater scrutiny from global regulators, policymakers and governments. Issues such as anti-money laundering rules for exchanges and wallets, the use of DeFi, crypto assets and property rights will all have to be addressed.'

'Finally, there is the question of who owns the metaverse.'

'Oh, that's easy. Just as nobody truly owns the Internet, no single person or company owns the metaverse. It's too big to be owned by any single entity. Just as in 1993 we couldn't tell what exactly the Internet was and how big it could become, the metaverse could be bigger than anything we have ever known.'

'So, I guess this is still a work in progress, correct?'

'Of course. We are still some time away before this becomes mainstream. Today, the most popular way to experience the metaverse is via a video game played on a VR headset. However, the metaverse is moving towards becoming the next iteration of the Internet, or Web3.

This "Open Metaverse" would be community-owned, community-governed, and a freely interoperable version that ensures privacy by design. However, we are likely decades away from mass adoption,' Srini said as they ended their discussion and got up to leave.

Takeaways

1. The metaverse is a computer-generated world where you can meet people, attend classes, play games, watch concerts, do your job, visit places, browse store shelves, etc.

2. Immersion, socialization, expressiveness and real-time interactivity are the key elements of the metaverse.

3. People are likely to have multiple identities in the metaverse—maybe as many as ten avatars per person—e.g., one for sports activities or games, another for school work, another for music concerts. Digital property in the metaverse will likely span skins, avatars, emotes, NFTs, fungible tokens and collectibles, among others.

4. Although there are a number of large tech companies as well as start-ups working on the metaverse, mass adoption may still be decades away as a high level of investment will be needed in areas such as computational resources, storage, network infrastructure, consumer hardware and game development platforms.

CHAPTER 23

Marathon or Sprint: Start-ups and Angel Investing

Training and Preparation—Kipchoge vs Bolt

Early on a Sunday morning, Siddharth went on a long run of twenty-one km with his marathon training group. After he came back home, his legs felt tired, but mentally, he felt energized. After his long runs, he always felt a sense of accomplishment.

His family had already finished their breakfast. Siddharth's father was reading the newspaper while his mom was reading a religious text. Shraddha was listening to some songs on their Echo Dot while doing some house cleaning and their daughter, Amayra, was doing her homework. Siddharth went to freshen up.

As he sat at the dining table for breakfast and had his cup of tea, he announced, 'You know, Kipchoge has set a new world record at the Berlin marathon.' He had checked the results online.

There was no response from anyone. His dad continued to read his newspaper resolutely while his mom brought fresh idlis to the table. Shraddha finally gave him a smile and nodded but said nothing.

'Oh, that's nice. Isn't he the one whose training videos you keep watching on repeat?' Finally, their fourteen-year-old daughter Amayra acknowledged him as she took a break from her homework and came and sat next to him at the dining table to give him company.

'Absolutely right, he's the one,' Siddharth was happy that at least someone in his family knew what he was talking about. He told her about Kipchoge's plans to win all six of the World Marathon Majors as well as the Olympics in 2024.

'But do you know what he said after the marathon?' he asked her.

'What?' asked Amayra.

'He said, "I aim for one thing at a time." He is very disciplined and that's the secret to his success. His mantra in life is, "Discipline sets you free." Do you know Kipchoge's training regime?'

'No, dad. But I am sure it must be intense.'

'Well, while training, he stays away from his family at a training camp with other runners from Monday morning to Saturday morning. He runs every day, alternating between fast and easy runs, speed workouts and interval training, and covers more than 200 km every week. He has a simple diet and gets proper sleep, rest and recovery. And not only that, he is extremely humble.'

'Humble? Exactly what do you mean?'

'Despite being a star athlete, he cleans the camp along with the other runners. He also makes it a point to spend the weekend with his family and helps his kids with their homework. That's why I like Kipchoge and his marathon running. He is a role model and teaches you the value of discipline. And discipline is what leads to success whether it's in marathons, in the investments-related work I do, in your studies, or anything else for that matter,' said Siddharth as his mom served him piping hot idlis.

'Ma, what are you doing? I am talking of discipline and you are piling my plate with idlis. I can't eat so many! I need to be a bit disciplined about my diet.'

'Don't worry, beta. Just eat. You run marathons. You need the energy,' his mom ignored his pleadings as Shraddha and Amayra broke into laughter. It was a common interaction between Siddharth and his mom at every breakfast, lunch and dinner at home.

Siddharth enjoyed the hot idlis with tasty coconut chutney and spicy sambhar. He needed the carbohydrates after his long run.

'By the way, would you like to join me on my next run?' Siddharth asked Amayra.

'No thanks, dad. Who has the time for long runs? You know I run the 100-metre sprint and am part of my school's 4x100-metre relay team, right? I prefer sprinting to running marathons. And I am more of a Usain Bolt fan. Our generation wants speed and quick results, dad.'

'Yes, how can I forget? Your team won the 4x100-metres relay in the interschool championship. And, of course, I am also a fan of Usain Bolt. But I hope your generation knows that quick results don't come just like that. That's why I gave you Kipchoge's example. And I am sure even Bolt had to be very disciplined in his training.'

'Of course, I know that, dad. Even I have done some research on Bolt's training routine. Do you know that, in addition to running short sprints during training, to maintain his edge, Bolt used to hit the gym for ninety-minute workouts every day?'

'Oh, really! That's news to me. I didn't know that he did such strenuous workouts. Why did he need to do that in addition to sprint training?'

'The workouts were geared toward developing explosiveness in his muscles while maintaining his lean physique. His workouts were strong and super-intense, and primarily included exercises that improved speed and agility. Bolt practised sprinting on the track every day after his gym session.'

'Wow. You really seem to have done your research!'

'Yes, dad, I have learnt it from you. But, you are right. Whether it is marathon running or sprinting, nothing is easy. Bolt trained very hard every single day and followed a strict diet to be the world's best at his game.'

'It seems to me that just like Kipchoge, Bolt's fitness plan also was both methodological and consistent.'

'Absolutely. It was his rigorous routine that helped him build the stability required to hit a top speed close to 45 km per hour.'

'So, what drove Bolt?'

'"I don't want to come in second"—that's what he said in an interview. You know, Bolt won eight gold medals in three Olympics, and he ran for less than 115 seconds on the track, earning almost 120 million dollars. That's what sprinting is about.'

'Yes, but for those two minutes, he trained for twenty years. That's investment. So, you should always think long-term. Patience pays.'

'I was sure you would bring in your investment angle somewhere,' Shraddha, who was listening intently to Siddharth and Amayra's discussion the entire time, jumped in. 'So, what worked for both Kipchoge and Bolt?'

'It's their training over a long period of time. Nothing comes easy,' Siddharth responded.

'Here's a quote from Bolt: "I trained four years to run nine seconds and people give up when they don't see results in two months,"' Amayra read from her phone.

'The key learning for us here is that whether it's finishing a marathon or running a quick sprint, it's the training and preparation over the years that counts. Nothing is quick,' Siddharth reiterated as he finished his breakfast and they got up from the dining table.

Marathon or Sprint

That evening, Siddharth and his family went to his uncle's home for dinner. His uncle, Manohar, was an out-and-out risk-taker. He had quit his job at a leading IT services company at the prime of his career to start his own software company. He was doing reasonably well and liked to move fast.

Siddharth loved to get an understanding of different sectors and companies. So, he asked a lot of questions regarding the technology sector that Manohar was happy to answer.

After dinner, the topic changed to what Siddharth was up to. Siddharth told Manohar about how he was guiding his clients to maintain proper asset allocation and follow the basic principles of financial planning. They spoke about investing in mutual funds and stocks as well as new avenues such as cryptocurrencies, NFTs and the metaverse. Siddharth also told him how he likened the journey of financial independence to running a marathon.

'Oh, I am sure you would do that given that you like to run marathons,' Manohar laughed.

'Yes, I do. It just makes things more credible and tangible,' Siddharth replied with a smile.

'That may be true for most people, Siddharth, but not for everyone. You know, I'd prefer to sprint towards achieving financial independence rather than running a long marathon. Why don't you tell me how I can do that?'

'What you are saying is true. But, whether it's running a marathon or a sprint, it requires proper planning, preparation and disciplined training,' Siddharth explained, as he gave Manohar an example of Eliud Kipchoge and Usain Bolt which he had discussed earlier in the day with his family at home. 'Both Kipchoge and Bolt needed to put in decades of training to achieve success. It's just that in the end, one runs what seems like a long marathon and the other runs what seems like a quick sprint.'

'Hmm. What you are saying makes sense. There is no magic wand or shortcut to success. But I can always choose to train for the sprint instead of a marathon, correct?'

'Absolutely.'

'So, what would it mean in the investment context?'

'It would mean being in a position to take more risk with the expectation of a higher reward.'

'Exactly. That was my point, Siddharth. Let me be more specific. You talk about mutual funds, which have been around as an investment option for a long time now. But, now there are so many start-ups that are doing a lot of innovation in different fields. We can invest in them too, right? Do you look at the start-up world at all?'

'Yes, you are right. We have a new asset class in angel investing and venture funding, wherein we can invest in start-ups and unlisted companies. But they are all high-risk and may not be suitable for everyone.'

'That's true. But the situation in India has changed completely in the last two years and if your clients are not investing in this segment, then they are missing out. Do you know that one in every eight new companies in India today is a start-up?'

'I was not aware of this.'

Start-Up Culture

'The start-up culture is emerging into the mainstream now. Shows like *Shark Tank*, IPOs of some new-age start-ups, and the rise of unicorns, which are start-ups that have crossed a valuation of $1 billion, have made start-ups front-page stuff.'

'I agree. I have read that huge value has been created in the start-up ecosystem and India now has more than 100 unicorns.'

'That's true. India's venture capital sector had its coming-out party in 2021 with a sudden jump in domestic money from high-net-worth individuals, family offices and local institutions coming in.'

'But from what I understand, things have cooled down relatively now as central banks across the world have started raising rates and reducing liquidity from the financial system. In fact, I read that some start-up founders have started talking of a "funding winter" and have started focusing on cutting costs.'

'That's true. But it only means that the best and most worthy start-ups will survive. And as you say, we should focus on the long-term. From that perspective, I still find start-ups to be the most promising segment for investment. I myself have been investing in a few start-ups over the past few years. And I have been fortunate to have a couple of good exits at a much higher valuation than when I invested in the start-ups.'

'Wow. That's amazing. I have been doing some research and have spoken to a few folks about investing in start-ups but there's just so much happening that it can be difficult to keep track. Since you are running your own company and are also a successful start-up investor, it would be great to discuss this asset class with you and understand your perspective.'

'Sure. Most of my time goes into running my own company. But I am part of a start-up founders' group. We keep discussing what's happening in the start-up world both in India and globally, and exchanging investment ideas and leads. It benefits everyone.'

'Great. Let's start from the basics then. What do you think has led to the increasing prevalence of start-ups globally and in India?'

Digital Transformation—The Key Driver

'See, the world is changing rapidly driven by digital transformation,' Manohar started. 'We are seeing a convergence of new technologies, including cloud computing, big data, artificial intelligence and the Internet of Things (IoT). They can be used to extract, store and analyse large amounts of data. These technologies did not exist till a few years ago but today, the availability of cheap data storage, inexpensive sensors and small-sized supercomputers run by artificial intelligence, or AI, algorithms, all interconnected by fast networks, has changed the backdrop completely. Creating a start-up has become much easier in this environment. And even large organizations are using this infrastructure to transform themselves into real-time adaptive enterprises.'

'Yes, I have also been reading off and on about these new technologies,' Siddharth nodded. 'Together, these will enable us to develop new applications and address problems in a way that we couldn't think of a few years ago, right?'

'Exactly. Analytics and predictions will become much more accurate. That is what digital transformation is all about,' Manohar continued. 'But that's not all. Digital transformation is leading to the demise of many existing companies and the creation of new kinds of companies. For example, in telecom we have seen a transition from telegraph to telephone to cell phone to smartphone. It's tough to even imagine now how we used to live earlier without a smartphone. And it's not just phone calling that has been disrupted. The smartphone has killed many other products. For example, even cameras have become redundant as everyone just uses their smartphone to click pictures and even videos now. A lot of innovations are essentially just apps on our phones.'

'Similarly, in digital entertainment, we have moved from theatres to video cassette to DVD to OTT streaming,' Siddharth pointed out. 'Most of us watch a lot of content on YouTube, Netflix, Amazon Prime,

Disney Hotstar or Sony Liv and other such platforms now. By analysing our content-viewing patterns, these platforms are now able to understand what we like and that enables them to produce and deliver more of such content. Even in our home, TV time has reduced and it's been some time since we have gone to watch a movie in a theatre.'

'Bang on. All our social media apps like YouTube, Instagram, Facebook, WhatsApp, Twitter, LinkedIn, Pinterest, etc., where we spend most of our time online, are cloud-based platforms. Music, for example, is being delivered through cloud-based services such as Spotify and Apple Music. Cloud-based streaming services such as Netflix and Amazon Prime Video are growing rapidly. And ride-sharing services like Uber and Ola wouldn't exist without the cloud. All these companies also use big data technology to store large amounts of data on their customers and then use AI algorithms to analyse the data and recommend products and services to customers.'

'Okay. So where is all this headed?'

'Well, everything from shopping, entertainment and education to financial solutions and healthcare is moving online at a rapid pace in India and globally.'

'I guess a confluence of factors is driving this transition, such as rising smartphone and Internet penetration, a gamut of enabling platforms and adoption of digital transactions. India's smartphone users are projected to rise from around 550 million now to around 850 million by 2025, comparable to China's current user base.'

'Yes. But this is just the starting point. Building on that, India has been fast and forward-looking in building a robust stack of digital platforms. The JAM trinity—Jan Dhan bank account, Aadhaar-based identification or e-KYC and Mobile—have laid the foundation. On top of that, we have seen platforms like the Unified Payments Interface or UPI, account aggregators, GST data, OCEN, which is the Open Credit Enablement Network, and ONDC—the Open Network for Digital Commerce, which have been developed by central agencies.'

'And to top it off, abundant private capital and talent have helped to customize these platforms for users, with Covid giving a fillip to user adoption.'

'Yes. The environment was just right for launching start-ups into orbit.'

'In India, which sectors have you seen start-ups to be more prevalent in? That would be good to understand,' said Siddharth.

'Good question. Let's discuss that in detail,' Manohar replied. 'But let's have some dessert first,' he said, as handed over a bowl of gulab jamuns to Siddharth.

Takeaways

1. Whether it's finishing a marathon or running a quick sprint, it's the training and preparation over the years that count. Nothing is quick.
2. Angel investing and venture funding is a new asset class wherein we can invest in start-ups and unlisted

companies. But these are all high-risk and may not be suitable for everyone.

3. The start-up culture is emerging into the mainstream in India now. Shows like *Shark Tank*, IPOs of some new-age start-ups and the rise of unicorns, which are start-ups that have crossed a valuation of $1 billion, have made start-ups front-page stuff.

4. Digital transformation, which involves the convergence of new technologies, including cloud computing, big data, artificial intelligence and the Internet of Things (IoT) is a key driver for the launch of new start-ups.

24

Future Road Map: Start-up Themes

'Half the start-ups in India belong to just five sectors: e-commerce, fintech, edtech, healthtech and enterprise SaaS, which stands for software as a service,' Manohar continued. 'These are the most popular sectors targeted by start-up founders.'

'Let's start with e-commerce, then,' Siddharth requested him. 'Everyone has adopted it now for the convenience it provides.'

E-commerce

'Yes, when it comes to shopping, we are moving from bricks to clicks with e-commerce. A few of the start-ups in this space have scaled up significantly over the past decade even as others have failed. Now, even large conglomerate groups in India are entering this space with their heft. And that's not all. There's a large number of direct-to-consumer (D2C) brands that are coming up. They just bypass intermediaries, such as wholesalers and retailers, and sell directly to consumers online. In the future, they could be challengers to established brands. '

'You are right. At my home, three generations— my mother, my wife and my daughter—are now very comfortable ordering stuff online and they are also open to experimenting with these new D2C brands. And I am seeing the same with others too, across age and income groups.'

'Yes. But we are now moving beyond basic e-commerce on a website or app to social commerce wherein transactions happen in the social media app itself. Social media is moving beyond just the discovery of products to enabling users to complete the entire purchase process without leaving the app. And that's not all. We are now moving to quick commerce with promises of ten-minute delivery. The launch of ONDC could also cause significant disruption in this space.'

'Do you know anyone who has invested in these social commerce and quick commerce start-ups?'

'Of course, some of my friends have invested in them. But that's not all. In the next few years, we will see VR and AR integrated into our shopping experience where, for example, we can try out some piece of apparel virtually to see how we look before we buy it.'

'That would be cool. Fintech is also a term I hear a lot these days. What does that entail?'

Fintech

'Fintech is an all-encompassing term that covers the technology and innovation that is disrupting how financial services such as banking, lending, payments, insurance, investments, wealth management, etc. are delivered to customers.'

'Yes. I have heard of neobanks that are gaining prominence as platforms to digitize banking or bank-like services for millennials and small and mid-sized businesses. One neobank even approached me to open an account saying that they would give me a credit card but with Amayra's name so that she could start using it and learn how to track her expenses and manage her spending. These neobanks want to catch their customers when they are young.'

'At the same time, UPI is becoming truly universal and is disrupting the payments space. UPI is gaining widespread adoption by retailers, given both ease of payments as well as the zero commission, and the zero Merchant Discount Rate or MDR regime mandated by the government.'

'No wonder UPI now accounts for more than 50 per cent of retail digital payments and is an order of magnitude higher than debit plus credit card transactions. And it's so easy. Everyone from large retailers, neighbourhood kirana stores and roadside vendors now use UPI. It's so streamlined that not just Shraddha and I but even mom and dad are comfortable using UPI now. Even Amayra finds that very convenient.'

'Lending to individuals and small and mid-sized businesses is another segment seeing a lot of disruption led by customized loan products like 'Buy Now Pay Later', new ways of underwriting using alternative credit-decisioning algorithms based on AI, and the advent of India Stack with OCEN, Sahay, Public Credit Registry or PCR, account aggregators and Aadhaar, among others.'

'I am sure we will see a lot of innovation and disruption in the financial services space going forward. Edtech is also in the news a lot these days, right?'

Edtech

'Yes. I am seeing many such developments in the education sector too, where technology is being used to deliver lessons online or in a hybrid mode. That's called edtech. And it's not just about online lectures and Q and A sessions or recorded videos any more. Very soon, we are going to see VR and AR embedded in the learning material.'

'Sure. During Covid, students got used to online classes. And although they have now started attending their school or college offline, online education will likely continue to play a key role to complement offline classes. In my own home, I am seeing that although Amayra prefers to go to school for the interaction with her classmates and teachers, she sometimes prefers to attend some classes online as it is convenient and saves time. I have also seen her searching for YouTube videos on topics where she is stuck and needs some help.'

'Yes. Many edtech companies have scaled up quickly during Covid and become unicorns.'

'Indian families always place a premium on their kids' education and will always be willing to try new solutions that may give their kids an edge in an environment of hyper-competition. This space is bound to do well.'

'That's true. But edtech companies are not restricted to high school students or those studying for competitive exams only. Now, they have marked their presence in skilling and certification for professionals too. Some are even combining education and entertainment to conduct online classes for people wanting to master their hobbies or passions.'

'That's interesting. I wasn't aware of it. Edtech is definitely a space worth watching. Let's talk about healthtech next.'

Healthtech

'Just like fintech, healthtech is an all-encompassing term used for technology and innovation used to deliver healthcare services outside the hospital or doctor's office. It covers various segments, such as tele-medicine, digital devices and wearables, development of new vaccines, online platforms for ordering medicines, healthcare products, etc.'

'If I understand it right, these start-ups focus on disease symptoms tracking, disease testing and diagnostics, tele-medicine, biopharmaceutical research and medical supplies.'

'Correct. There's really innovative work going on in AI-powered drug discovery and assistive technologies using virtual or augmented reality, AI and robotics to assist persons with disabilities, and anti-ageing and gene therapy to find a cure for cancer, HIV and heart disease. Some start-ups are developing software and hardware solutions to empower individuals to take better care of their mental health and enable practitioners to better monitor the mental health of their patients.'

'Some of these could be revolutionary. Shraddha got a fitness tracking watch as a birthday gift. And I got one too, to wear on my training runs and track key parameters such as my heart rate, fitness level and recovery rate. I am finding it to be really useful in my training runs. I am sure we will see some revolutionary products in the healthtech space over the next decade. Lastly, what are some of the sub-segments in enterprise SaaS?'

Enterprise SaaS

'Here, there are multiple business models, such as book-keeping and accounting services for small and mid-sized businesses, online platforms for teachers and creators to offer classes, marketplaces to help creators and educators sell content to students, as well as marketplaces to help doctors sell services to patients, etc.'

'We've covered the five sectors of e-commerce, edtech, fintech, healthtech and enterprise SaaS. Are there any other sectors you find interesting?'

Electric Vehicles

'In personal transportation, we have made a leap from horse carriages to cars with internal combustion engines or ICE to electric vehicles or EVs. We have already seen some electric two-wheelers and four-wheelers in India too.'

'For most of us, our next vehicle is likely to be an electric vehicle. I think the EV infrastructure in India will evolve quickly over the next decade.'

'Correct. We should note that 85 per cent of vehicles sold in India are two-wheelers and three-wheelers. Given that smaller and simpler batteries suffice for them, as well as the desire for fuel savings from less-affluent riders and operators, and finally government incentives, the environment is in place for driving faster growth of EVs over traditional, or ICE, vehicles. And there are a number of start-ups in this space in India that are racing to provide affordable products.'

'There are still some teething issues in this space with news reports of some electric scooters catching fire spontaneously, correct?'

'Yes. The start-up world is all about "move fast, fail fast, and make improvements in the next version". But that may not always work, especially when human lives are involved.'

'Absolutely. To avoid such issues, the government is now coming out with more stringent regulations on testing and quality control, especially for the batteries, which are the most important component of an electric vehicle.'

'That is the need of the hour. But globally, the world is also working on autonomous vehicles where vehicles will drive themselves and drivers may not be required. There are a number of advanced trials happening in the US and other countries. And although it will take some time for these technologies to come to India, it's only a matter of time.'

'One can only imagine the issues that can come up and the regulations needed in this case.'

'Yes. That will be a bone of contention. Well, we have covered the five key sectors for Indian start-ups as well as electric vehicles. But, there are also many other interesting segments such as gaming and e-sports, the metaverse, AI and machine learning, robotics and automation, sustainability and green energy, logistics, agritech, plant-based foods, sharing economy, etc.'

'What do you mean by sharing economy?'

'It is essentially Uberification across transport, travel and hospitality, leisure and work, food, retail and other sectors wherein one doesn't need to own an asset but can access it on an as-needed basis. A good example of this would be start-ups in the hospitality sector that don't own any hotels themselves.'

'Okay, Manohar. Clearly, there's a lot more to talk about. But we would end up discussing this for the rest of the night. And Shraddha is already indicating to me that it's getting late.'

'You are right, Siddharth. That is what happens when I meet my start-up founder friends too. There are just so many new ideas and start-ups coming up that we end up losing track of time. But I find it very energizing. So, we can continue our discussion for a few more minutes.'

Takeaways

1. E-commerce, fintech, edtech, healthtech and enterprise SaaS (Software as a Service) are the most popular themes for start-ups in India.
2. Electric vehicles, sustainability and green energy are also seeing a lot of interest.
3. Gaming and e-sports, the metaverse, AI and machine learning, robotics and automation, logistics, agritech, plant-based foods, sharing economy, etc., are interesting areas for the future.

25

A Framework for Investing in Start-ups

'The key question that remains is, how can interested investors invest in start-ups?' Siddharth questioned Manohar.

'Well, there are multiple ways. In some cases, a few good friends and I have invested directly in start-ups where we had a good connect with the founders. In other cases, we have invested through angel investing networks, some of which also have dedicated funds. Some of my friends who have a large enough capital base to invest have also invested in larger and more established VC, that's venture capital, funds.'

'I have heard about VC funds earlier but angel investing networks are something new. Could you explain how they work? Some of my clients could be interested.'

'Sure, angel investing networks have democratized early-stage investments. So, not just high-net-worth individuals, but even salaried and professional individuals can invest in this asset class if they meet the minimum net worth and experience criteria mandated by the regulators. There are a number of angel investing networks in India. One can become a member by paying an annual fee. The angel investing networks provide access and opportunity to invest small amounts, as low as Rs 2 to 2.5 lakh in a single start-up. So one can build a portfolio of start-ups in a process-based manner.'

'That's good. Getting access to start-ups itself is a roadblock for most investors. And, it looks as though angel investing networks solve that problem.'

'Right. Another advantage is that it's a streamlined process and makes things simple for investors. These networks do their independent diligence on start-ups that are looking to raise capital. The few start-ups that pass their standards then are given an opportunity to pitch to the network members who are interested in knowing more. And members who find any start-up to be a convincing opportunity can then do some more diligence on their own and decide to invest in it for a small equity stake.'

'But these are all very early stage investments, right? So, is there enough information to make a decision?'

'You are right. Angel investment is about discovering promising start-ups at very early stages and funding them in exchange for equity. Most of the time, start-ups at this stage may just be able to show some customer traction with minimal revenue and some may not even have reached that stage. Therefore, the criterion for investing involves having a strong belief in the founders or the product and evaluating the market opportunity and the business idea's potential, strategy, product viability, etc. Of course, some start-ups do come for additional rounds of funding too after getting more traction in the market.'

'Is there a minimum or maximum amount that one can invest in a start-up?'

'The investment can be as low as Rs 2 to 2.5 lakh or as high as a few crores depending on the risk-taking capacity of the investor. Some networks have also launched their own alternative investment fund (AIF) and members can only invest through these funds.'

'And how can members track how their investments are doing?'

'Good question. The angel investing networks have a process in place so that start-ups provide regular updates to members who have invested in them. And members can invest in follow-on rounds too if the start-up executes well and reaches the next stage of funding.'

'Okay. But the risk is also quite high, correct? Angel investors typically invest in the initial rounds when the start-ups are still quite small and potentially unproven.'

'Yes. Start-ups at this stage are looking to scale up their business to a size where a VC fund will find them appealing to invest in. They need funds to invest in hiring talent, R and D for product development, manufacturing products, marketing, etc.'

'And many start-ups do not succeed in this effort, correct?'

'Absolutely. Out of ten start-ups at this stage, five may fail completely, three or four may turn out to be average, and one or two may become hugely successful. The exit event usually occurs within a three- to five-year period but could be earlier as well. The point is that one or two successful investments can more than make up for the failures. But there are no guarantees.'

'So, it's important to allocate just a small portion, say 5 per cent of one's overall portfolio to angel investing, if at all based on one's risk appetite, then follow a portfolio approach and diversify across multiple start-ups. One can't just invest in a couple of start-ups and expect to get good returns.'

'Yes. Some people call it the "spray-and-pray" approach. How would you compare investing in start-ups versus investing in mutual funds, which you normally recommend to your clients?'

Diversification in Start-Up Investing

'Well, on the face of it, the start-up investing world seems very different from investing in mutual funds and listed stocks as the risk is much higher and it's an illiquid asset class, which means that investors cannot just exit when they want. However, there are some basic investment and behavioural principles that straddle both these worlds.'

'Oh, is that so? Do tell me more.'

'I think there are three key principles that can help us become better investors in start-ups.'

20-Slot Rule

'As Warren Buffett says, let's think we have a ticket with only twenty slots in it. So, we have twenty punches—representing all the start-up investments that we get to make in a fixed period of time, say three years.

'Under these rules, we'd start thinking really carefully about what we should do. We'll invest only in those start-ups that we really think have high potential and we'd avoid the rest. So, chances are, we'd do much better than just following a spray-and-pray approach and ending up with a random collection of start-ups.'

'Sure, but how can we do this in practice?'

'Step 1 is to fix the quantum of money we'd like to invest in start-ups over a certain period of time. Let's say this is Rs 50 lakh over three years.

'Step 2 then is to divide this quantum into twenty smaller bites. So, we break up our Rs 50 lakh into twenty bites of Rs 2.5 lakh each.

'Step 3 is to be disciplined about making only these twenty bite-sized investments across start-ups in first rounds, follow-on rounds, etc.

'Note that with this approach, we may end up investing in anywhere between ten to twenty start-ups, which is a good number. After all, we need to track the investments we have made too. Any number higher than this will make it difficult to monitor our investments.'

'That makes sense. The next question then is how to build a well-rounded portfolio with these ten to twenty investments.'

'That's where the principle of asset allocation and diversification comes into the picture.'

Diversification

'There are many different aspects to diversification beyond just the number of start-ups we invest in.

'**a. Different industries or sectors:** Even though our own expertise may be in one sector, say retail, we should not restrict our investments only to retail and e-commerce but also evaluate start-ups in other sectors. Different sectors perform well during different periods of the business cycle. So even if one start-up in our portfolio is not doing well because the sector it belongs to is in a slowdown, some other start-up in another sector may do well and balance things out.'

'Even within one sector like technology, which has a number of sub-themes like enterprise SaaS, artificial intelligence and machine learning (AI-ML), blockchain, robotics and automation, etc., which can disrupt established business in various sectors, it would be advisable to diversify across sub-themes and not just in one sub-theme like enterprise SaaS.'

'**b. Different stages of development:** It is important to have start-ups of different vintage to reduce the risk of failure. Here, we should look to have some very early-stage companies with longer timelines and higher risk but with potentially higher returns as well as some later-stage companies, which we can expect to exit sooner and get our capital back with modest returns.'

'**c. Different types of founders/teams:** We should aim for diversity in social, educational, gender and cultural backgrounds in our overall portfolio to diversify the people risk. This means we shouldn't go with all late-career entrepreneurs any more than we should go with all millennials as CEOs. We don't want all men or all women. We don't want all engineers or all marketing professionals. We want to make sure that we invest in the right mix of people and that each entrepreneur or team has the appropriate skills for the opportunity at hand.'

'**d. Different types of underlying risks:** Some start-ups can end up facing "execution" type risks in fixable areas like go-to-market strategy, and choice of vertical or marketing strategy while others can face more fundamental risks, such as technical or scientific risk. While we may have both types in our portfolio, in general, start-ups with execution type risks may have a better chance of successfully overcoming them.'

'Hmm. This is a very useful framework to keep in mind. I have been investing in start-ups but didn't follow a structured thought process as you have outlined.'

'Yes. But there's a final aspect to keep in mind. We should bear in mind that the three most important words in investing, whether in public markets or in start-ups, are "margin of safety".'

'What is that?'

Margin of Safety

'Since start-ups are at an early stage in their lifecycle, there isn't much of a track record to establish their valuation with high confidence. So, if a deal seems over-priced or if it seems priced for perfect execution with no room for error, then the risk of failure goes up and it's best to walk away. Remember that if you invest in a start-up at a high valuation, the chances of your investment becoming a multibagger can diminish significantly. Always keep in mind that investing in start-ups is a high-risk, high-return affair. So, unless you give yourself a chance to earn a significant return by investing at a relatively low valuation, your investment may not compensate for the risk you are taking.

'Whether it's a publicly traded stock or a start-up, don't worry about missing a great investment. Another one will follow.'

'Siddharth, I wish we had this discussion earlier. I can see that you have put some thought into this,' Manohar said, after listening to Siddharth outlining his start-up investing framework. 'I would have made much better investment choices for my start-up portfolio instead of just following a spray-and-pray approach.'

'Yes, we should have discussed this earlier, Manohar. I learnt so many new aspects of start-ups that I was not aware of earlier. I can guide my clients in a better way now,' said Siddharth as they ended their discussion.

Takeaways

1. Angel investing networks have democratized early-stage investments. So, not just high-net-worth individuals but even salaried and professional individuals can invest in this asset class if they meet minimum net worth and experience criteria.

2. Since this is a high-risk investment, it's important to allocate just a small portion, say 5 per cent of one's overall portfolio to angel investing, if at all, then follow a portfolio approach and diversify across multiple start-ups.

3. Basic principles to keep in mind are the 20-slot rule, diversifying across start-ups in different themes and sectors, in different stages of development, with different types of founders/teams, and with different underlying risks.

4. It's important to have a margin of safety. If a deal seems over-priced or if it seems priced for perfect execution with no room for error, then the risk of failure goes up and it's best to walk away.

Conclusion

My wife was one of the first people to read this book. I found her in deep thought as she finished and put the book down.

'Did you like the book?' I asked her.

'You have explained key concepts really well. I wish I had known them earlier,' she replied.

'That's good to know. So, what are your takeaways from the book?'

'First is that money creates time. I never thought of it like that.

'Second, financial independence is important because it gives us the ability to live our life on our own terms and choose to do only those things that make us happy.

'Third, financial independence is not just about delayed gratification and saving money. That's just the first step. It's about investing our savings wisely to generate passive income and grow our wealth. I now understand asset allocation and the five key principles of financial planning, namely, savings before expenses, compound interest, emergency fund, market risk and inflation. Also, I now have some knowledge about available investment solutions and products such as mutual funds, index funds and ETFs as well as the new world of blockchain, crypto, NFTs, the metaverse and investing in start-ups.

'Fourth, the key is not to think of financial independence as a goal but as a marathon, which we need to enjoy. We are not competing with anyone but just need to cross the finish line in our own time.

'Fifth, preparation is everything for this journey and it would be beneficial to seek the services of an expert in the form of a financial adviser so that we don't make basic mistakes and end up with a mishap that spoils our journey.'

'Wow. I couldn't have summarized it better. You have grasped the key concepts really well.'

'You know, I'd like to start my journey to financial independence too,' she said. 'My savings are being eaten away by inflation,' she added with some disappointment. 'But I have understood the five basic principles of financial planning now and would like to apply them.'

'Oh, so after nineteen years of marriage in which you put your hard-earned savings only in FDs, you finally saw the light!' I pulled her leg.

'Well, it's better late than never,' she said. 'I understand the importance of proper asset allocation now and would like to build a diversified portfolio as you have suggested in your book. Can you give me some suggestions?'

'Wow. That's great, welcome to the club!' I told her with some pride as I shortlisted a few investment options for her to choose from. 'If you are disciplined with your investments, you'll be able to tap-dance your way to financial independence,' I informed her.

'That's good to know,' she seemed relieved. 'I'd also like to do a crypto transaction, just to understand how it works. It seems interesting,' she added, as I almost fell out of my chair.

'Hold on. Let's go step by step. Get the basics right first and then you can think about crypto,' I advised her.

'Relax. I just wanted to see your reaction,' she said with a smile.

'Does this also mean that you trust me now?' I ventured further.

'Don't push your luck. Let's see how far your advice takes me in my journey and then I'll decide,' she responded with a smile. 'And as you have said, it's a marathon and it's going to be a long one. But I am happy that you will be along with me on this journey . . .'

Acknowledgements

The entire community of investors, independent financial advisers, and mutual fund distributors has my heartfelt gratitude. My interactions with them over the past few years gave me an all-round perspective on the mindset of investors. It got me thinking about how I could assist investors on their financial independence journey and gave me the raw material to write my book.

There are a number of role models from whom I have learnt about the science and art of investing, its pitfalls and how best to avoid them, and how to communicate with investors. This gave me the confidence to think of potential solutions to the problems investors face in their journey and attempt to communicate my ideas in a simple and entertaining manner.

Warren Buffet, whom I had the good fortune to meet in person when I was doing my MBA at Wharton, is foremost among my role models. Meeting him kindled a lifelong love of investing in me and remembering his humility and kindness keeps me grounded every day.

That meeting led me to learn from the works of Benjamin Graham, Charlie Munger, Peter Lynch,

Howard Marks, Mohnish Pabrai, Gautam Baid and Saurabh Mukherjea, to name a few.

And of course, I am fortunate to work closely with A. Balasubramanian, Mahesh Patil, and K.S. Rao—CEO, CIO and head of investor education, respectively, at Aditya Birla Sun Life AMC Ltd as well as the entire investments team there.

Sessions with Anand Deshpande and Gautam Chhugani helped me overcome my apprehension and get a better understanding of the new world of crypto, blockchains, NFTs and the metaverse.

My family was the catalyst that finally got me to sit down and pen my thoughts. I would like to thank my daughter, Niyati, my wife, Roopa, my sisters, Lata and Geeta, and my mom for giving me constant motivation and keeping my spirits up during my journey of writing this book.

My friends—especially from St. Patrick's High School, IIT Bombay and Wharton, relatives and colleagues also encouraged me to write and gave a boost to my confidence.

It has been my privilege to work with Radhika Marwah and her team at Penguin Random House India. Their inputs have been instrumental to get this book in its present shape. My sincere appreciation to Radhika for her support and guidance, and to Ralph Rebello for his attention to detail and sharp-eyed inputs to refine the book.

A very special thanks to Shiv Shivakumar, my boss in my previous role, for penning the foreword. He has always been available for me and has always encouraged and supported me in my endeavours.

Since I had my own family members, relatives and friends as the target audience when I wrote this book, I requested them to read a draft. Their feedback made me realize that I had taken investors' understanding of many concepts for granted. I had to put in more effort to simplify concepts and put things across in a way that they would find interesting to read.

I appreciate Gautam Baid, Saurabh Mukherjea, K.S. Rao, Rajesh Krishnamoorthy, Rohit Shah, Gajanan Bhat, Sanjay Khorate, Nikhil Gurjar, Vijay Pawnarkar, Unmesh Kulkarni and Ujjwal Kumar for taking the time to review the manuscript and share their feedback and inputs to make it better.

A special mention to Hirak Bhattacharjee and Jayaraj Kuttapan from the HR team and Hemanti Wadhwa from the compliance team at Aditya Birla Sun Life AMC Ltd for their support.

Finally, my gratitude to you and all the other readers. I hope the learnings from my book will help you in your journey to financial independence. Good luck!

Thank you.

Bibliography

Galloway, Jeff. *Run Walk Run*. jeffgalloway.com/training/run-walk/

Mahesh Nandurkar, Jefferies. *Modeling Retail Investor Behaviour*, 2022.

García, Héctor and Francesc Miralles. *Ikigai: The Japanese Secret to a Long and Happy Life*. Random House UK, 2017.

Brinston, Gary, Brian D. Singer and Gilbert L. Beebower. *Determinants of Portfolio Performance II, An Update. Financial Analysts Journal*, May–June 1991.

Graham, Benjamin. *The Intelligent Investor Revised Edition*. Harper Business, 2006.

Lynch, Peter. *One Up on Wall Street*. Simon & Schuster, 2000.

Deshpande, Anand. *Introduction to Crypto and Web3*, 2022.

Bernstein. *A Neophyte's Guide to Ethereum*, 2021.

Web3 – A Vision for a Decentralized Web. https://blog.cloudflare.com/what-is-web3/

'How Many Bitcoins Are There?', buybitcoinworldwide.com/how-many-bitcoins-are-there/

'Crypto Firms Say Thousands of Digital Currencies Will Collapse', cnbc.com/2022/06/03/crypto-firms-say-thousands-of-digital-currencies-will-collapse.html

Yugalabs Future and Roadmap, 2022.

Metaverse and Money: Decrypting the Future. Citi GPS, 2022.

Bernstein. *Metaverse Primer*, 2021.

Gayton, Nelson. *Marathon to the Metaverse*, 2022.

McKinsey. *Value Creation in the Metaverse*, 2022.

Walsh, Mike. 'What Leaders Need to Know about the Metaverse', 2022.

'What It Takes to Be a Kenyan Distance Running Champion.' https://worldathletics.org/be-active/performance/kenyan-distance-running-reasons-success

'Usain Bolt: Training Secrets of the World's Fastest Man.' https://www.gq.com/story/runner-usain-bolt-training-secrets-and-diet

'India's 100 Unicorn Startups—Today Marks a New Milestone for India's Startup Economy.' https://inc42.com/features/indias-100-unicorn-startups-today-marks-a-new-milestone-for-indias-startup-economy/

Siebel, Thomas. *Digital Transformation: Survive and Thrive in an Era of Mass Extinction*, 2019.

Indus Valley Annual Report 2022, Blume Ventures.